FINISHING TOUCHES

FINISHING TOUCHES

LINDA GRAY

CHARTWELL
BOOKS, INC.

Published in 1987 by
Chartwell Books, Inc.
A Division of Books Sales, Inc.
110 Enterprise Avenue
Secaucus, New Jersey 07094

© Octopus Books Limited 1987
All rights reserved

ISBN 1 55521 166 6

Editor: Wendy Lee
Art editor: Lisa Tai
Designer: Simon Loxley
Picture researcher: Angela Grant
Production controller: Peter Thompson
American consultant: Sarah Lifton
Illustrations: Hayward and Martin Limited

Typeset by Peter McDonald
12, The Embankment
Twickenham, Middlesex

Produced by Mandarin Publishers Limited
22a Westlands Road
Quarry Bay, Hong Kong

Printed in Hong Kong

CONTENTS

INTRODUCTION

The wallpaper's up, the carpet is down, and there's a smell of new paint in the air. All you need to do now is to move back the furniture and hang the curtains. Or is it?

Few of us feel truly at home until we've arranged pictures, ornaments and treasures to our satisfaction because they are what gives each room its warmth and individuality. Showcase houses and room displays may be good to look at but we recognize them for what they are – showcases for the latest furnishing products and ideas rather than real homes.

Finishing Touches sets out to show you how to combine the two, creating a home which is not only stylish but which suits, and reflects, your lifestyle. It contains ideas and information to give each room that vital finishing touch, whether you're looking for lighting, bedlinen or blinds, wanting to frame and display paintings, needing to camouflage decorating disasters, or trying to disguise furniture that's seen better days. Seeing the room and its contents in a different light is often all that's needed to begin the transformation. It's a process that's most easily done after redecoration when the room itself looks new but, as you will see, it's perfectly possible to improve an existing scheme and to find a look which suits both your lifestyle and your budget.

The first section of the book concentrates on analyzing your style, assessing your requirements, planning the different areas of your home and translating the concepts of colour, pattern and texture into practical room schemes. Later chapters will help you see where there's room for improvement and suggest ways of tackling problems. It's all designed to make your home more than a 'halfway' house, whether you want to complete a newly decorated room – or one you never *quite* got round to finishing.

PART ONE

AT HOME WITH STYLE

Even a book about endings must begin at the beginning, which is what this section is all about. It will help you identify your style and, as you'll need to consider your circumstances as well as your preferences, it helps you to define your needs too. The demands of the different areas of the house – the routeways, work rooms, living areas and private places – are also discussed. Finally, there's the excitement of choosing the colours which make your home come alive, ready and waiting for that Finishing Touch.

CHAPTER 1

Identifying your style

What is your favourite style? Is it traditional or modern? Romantic or classic? Casual or formal? And is it a style you want to live with, or simply one you like to see?

Your personal style is usually the one with which you feel most at home. If you like to live informally, surrounded by your possessions, you probably prefer a cosy, possibly traditional look, like that of an Edwardian villa or a country cottage. You may not be happy in an austere Oriental-style setting where every object counts, and those that don't contribute to the style are glaringly out of place. On the other hand, if you like spare, uncluttered interiors where everything that's not in use is stored behind closed doors, it's a mistake to furnish with open shelves which attract more ornaments than you knew you owned. Of course you can take inspiration from other types of setting and vary the theme of different rooms if you wish – but keep to the style you instinctively prefer for rooms where you can expect to spend most of your time, whether they are work rooms like the kitchen or those where you want to relax and unwind, such as the living room and bedroom.

These are also rooms where it's wise to be quite conservative in your choice of colours and furnishings, particularly if this is a long- rather than short-stay home. That doesn't mean dull! It's simply that bold colour schemes and daring decorative ideas may pall if you see too much of them. A striped, tented ceiling that looks splendid in a dining room may quickly lose its appeal in a room where you spend every evening, while the burgundy walls which add character to the bathroom might not be quite what you want in the kitchen. On the other hand, they might. Burgundy may turn out to be one of your favourite colours and one that you'd happily be surrounded by sitting, eating or sleeping. But it's wise to try out the more demanding schemes in smaller areas first – just in case.

To help pinpoint the style you prefer, here's a look at the contrasting types, with an indication of the accessories which sum up the style.

PERIOD STYLES

These divide into two main categories – the cottage, and the town or country house. The main difference is that while cottages are casual, the house is more formal in style and more likely to reflect the impact of furnishing fashion.

THE COUNTRY COTTAGE

This relies on simplicity for effect. The cottage style (known in the US as country style) is not mannered – it has simply evolved. Local materials are used to furnish the basic needs of the inhabitants, which is why thatched or slate roofs, stone floors, rush mats, whitewashed walls, exposed beams and ledge and brace doors have come to be associated with the English cottage. Although there are local variations, most cottages have thick walls and small windows to keep out the cold and in a true cottage the front door opens into the living room.

The cottage style is easily adapted to suit small modern houses and starter homes – and let's face it, these are often more comfortable to live in than the genuine cottage with its solid walls and cold stone flags. Choose patterns with care. Small sprig design wallpapers printed on a light ground give the effect of 'looking through' the design which increases the sense of space and looks especially pretty used on the walls and ceilings of attic bedrooms with dormer windows; they also add interest to boxy modern rooms. Remember that you'd be unlikely to find wallpaper in a traditional cottage because the plaster is too rough and the walls far from straight, so plain matt (flat-finish) walls often look best in cottage living rooms and kitchens. You can afford to add a discreet amount of pattern at the windows though traditionally, of course, these would have had shutters rather than curtains. Keep to pale colours, natural fibres and rough textures, and make sure that the furniture you choose is equally in keeping with the unsophisticated cottage style. Look for simple furniture in oak, elm, beech or pine rather than highly polished exotic hardwoods, and keep to small-scale sofas and armchairs with leather, tweed, chintz or plain cotton covers for a traditional look. Don't overdo the folksy charm! Remember that these homes belonged to ordinary working people with little to spend on decoration. For a more modern interpretation, look at interiors designed in England early this century by Voysey or Ambrose Heal which capture this style – albeit in houses that are rather larger than the average cottage. Choose loop or long-pile rugs or carpets.

This cottage has been adapted for modern living without detriment to its original charm. Beams and fireplace are painted white, rush mats are fitted wall-to-wall and china is used in place of pictures. Out goes the range, in go the baskets, flowers – and wine rack.

High ceilings and tall windows give this early nineteenth-century house its elegant proportions. The sofa table and neo-classical settee are antique but reproductions are available for those who can't stretch to the real thing.

Finishing touches

Doors should be ledge and brace, with simple latches (not Tudor or Jacobean style).
Windows should be in keeping, too. Restore shutters if appropriate in an old cottage. Choose cotton print curtains, or print or plain blinds.
Walls may be colour-washed or painted with matt emulsion (flat latex); sprig pattern wallpapers or borders look good in bedrooms if the walls are straight.
Floors are covered with coir (coconut fibre) mats or runners; or use twist pile carpet and quarry tiles.
Accessories could be watercolours, jugs of fresh or dried flowers, patterned plates displayed on the walls or on shelves, or patterned earthenware.

THE TOWN OR COUNTRY HOUSE

This is a grander affair and easier to date. If you wish to follow a period faithfully, don't neglect the fine detail which means so much.

Georgian and **Regency** houses (called **Colonial** and **Federal** in America) are a delight to furnish. Their graceful proportions usually dictate a formal, or at least symmetrical, furniture arrangement, and the deep windows let in plenty of natural light, lack of which is often a problem with other period

homes. These allowed the Georgians to use unexpectedly deep paint colours – milk chocolate and sage green was a favourite combination – and these shades, plus grey-blue and buff, look surprisingly effective on the walls of larger eighteenth- and early nineteenth-century homes.

This is one of the most widely copied of period styles, but remember that neo-Georgian houses are likely to have smaller rooms and lower ceilings than original ones, so adapt colour schemes and furnishing plans accordingly. Oriental fabrics and carpets are a good choice as these were imported from India and China in Georgian times (chintz is adapted from an Indian word for a multi-coloured fabric) and furniture should be light and delicate. Look for the style of Chippendale, Hepplewhite and Sheraton if you like antiques or reproduction, but don't be afraid of selecting avant-garde designs if you prefer these. The Georgian room is so well-balanced that it makes an equally effective showcase for very modern furniture and adventurous colour schemes.

Finishing touches

Doors should be panelled, with brass door handles and key plates.
Windows may take swag and tail window dressings or simple drapes. Use chintz, cotton satin or velvet, or swathe the window in sheer fabric for a modern interpretation of the classical look.
Walls are painted in matt emulsion (flat latex) in deep shades. Replace mouldings and ceiling decorations.
Floors may be covered by Oriental rugs over wood; velvet (velour) pile carpet looks good in a modern home.
Accessories could be Chinese vases, ginger jar lamps, pine or marble mantelpieces, framed silhouettes, sketches or quill work, gilt frames, mirrors, console tables, sofa tables, writing desks, balloon and long case clocks, china by Wedgwood, Spode and Royal Worcester in delicate contemporary designs. (Wedgwood's cream Queen's ware, designed for Queen Charlotte, black basalt and blue and green jasper ware are still in production today.)

Victorian and **American Victorian** houses are darker and heavier, but often more comfortable. The early nineteenth century offered little in the way of large pieces of upholstery besides the shallow settee and the chaise longue, but in a few decades deep sofas and well-padded chairs had come into their own. Carpets, cushions and drapes were thick and often busily patterned and colours dark rather than pale.

Today you may want to let more light into your nineteenth-century home by choosing pale tints for the walls, but rich colours look striking in less frequently used rooms or very dark halls and passageways. Victorian homes are often large enough to accommodate very large pieces of furniture, like the vast wardrobes and sideboards associated with this period, though you may prefer a less decorated look than the contemporary Gothic style which turned cupboards into facsimile cathedrals. Look at Edwardian (early twentieth century) reproduction designs, fast appreciating in value, if you want a lighter look. Boldly patterned wallpaper is associated with the Victorian style. Many William Morris and Cole wallpaper and fabrics sell successfully today, and not only for nineteenth-century homes. One word of caution: if your Victorian home is a small terraced (row) house or villa, take care when incorporating period details. Avoid large-scale designs which may overwhelm the rooms, and take inspiration from the simple cottage style if you wish to achieve the very best results.

Finishing touches
Doors should be panelled, with heavy brass or floral china door knobs, key fobs and finger plates.
Windows may be dressed with velvet or cotton satin drapes, lace curtains and pelmets (valances).
Walls may have floral or flock wallpaper, complete with mouldings and picture rails.
Floors may take chenille or Oriental rugs over boards or close carpeting.
Accessories could be decorated earthenware (look at contemporary designs by Coalport, Crown Derby, Minton and Royal Worcester), heavy gilt picture frames, landscapes and portraits in oils, tablecloths, tasselled cushions, mantel clocks in slate or dark wood, carriage clocks, tablecloths, cast iron fireplaces, traditional cross-head taps or faucets.

Edwardian (early twentieth century) homes were often influenced by Art Nouveau, a sinuous decorative style popular towards the end of the nineteenth century and revived in the 1960s. Look at Maw's tiles, traditional Liberty prints and Morris designs with their use of the S-shaped ogee motif to see how this was translated into furnishings. Though similar to Victorian homes, the Edwardian age saw the in-troduction of a lighter touch in home furnishings and an end to the more oppressive aspects of the Victorian style which preceded it.

Many fabrics and wallpapers and much ceramic and silverware today take their inspiration from Art Nouveau and this style adapts well to many houses built between the middle of the nineteenth century and the First World War. Art Nouveau furniture wasn't so successful, but designs like the Mackintosh chair and English Quaker- or American Shaker-inspired furniture, which forsook curves for simple lines, have become furnishing classics.

Finishing touches
Doors should be panelled, with brass or china door furniture (hardware).
Windows may take heavy drapes in velvet, chintz, or cotton satin, arranged to effect on brass or dark wood curtain poles.
Walls may feature William Morris or Cole wallpaper in contemporary designs or Art Nouveau patterns, with dados.
Floors are covered in plain fitted (wall-to-wall) carpet or, alternatively, by patterned squares over sanded and sealed boards.

Does it surprise you that this thoroughly modern room includes furnishings (like the Rietveld lounger chair) designed in the 1920s? The Bauhaus school's liking for chrome and glass, simple shapes and bright colours is reflected here by the furniture and Mondrian rug.

Squashy sofas, fringes, friezes and feathers are elements of glamorous thirties-style interiors which unite in this living room. It's decorated in the shade of pink characteristic of the period, complete with parlour palm.

Accessories could be Celtic-style Art Nouveau silverware (tableware, picture frames), Art Nouveau tiles, Liberty fabrics, floral loose covers, Tiffany-style lamps, bentwood furniture (which is, in fact, mid-nineteenth century but looks splendid with the Art Nouveau style).

The interiors of the **1920s and 1930s** owe a debt to two important movements – Bauhaus and Art Deco. The Bauhaus was a German school of architecture which concentrated on designs for mass-production using industrial processes and modern materials. Even today Bauhaus-inspired tubular steel and leather furniture looks avant-garde, and you'll find variants of Marcel Breuer's Wassily chair and Le Corbusier's chaise longue in many fashionable settings. Art Deco is popularly called 'Odeon' style in Britain because so many cinemas called Odeon display its offset geometric patterns, rising sun motifs and strident colour schemes. Art Deco furniture and accessories are more obvious period pieces than the Bauhaus designs with their architectural bias, but both styles show a clarity of style and colour made possible by the use of steel, glass and leather.

Brilliant white paint was first produced at the time of the First World War and, together with the invention of modern domestic appliances, created a vogue for the all-white room in the twenties and thirties. It's no more practical for most of us now than it was then but white walls, off-white woodwork, creamy curtains or blinds, light wood or chrome and glass tables and storage sum up this style and create the perfect background for sculptural seating and Art Deco china. Orange, yellow, black, pink, peach and turquoise, other colours popular at the time, also look effective.

Finishing touches
Doors should be twenties-style panelled with steel door furniture (hardware).
Windows may have silky curtains or Venetian blinds.
Walls should be painted with white or pastel emulsion (latex) paint.
Floors are covered in velvet-pile fitted (velour wall-to-wall) carpet or plain long-pile rugs.
Accessories may include Art Deco china and table lamps, thirties-style radios, club armchairs, fine chrome and glass furniture, wicker chairs, leather upholstery and fan-shaped wall lights.

MODERN INTERIORS
These often continue the style of the 1920s and 1930s by using simple shapes, abstract designs, bold colours and contemporary materials for impact. At the same time, nostalgia has led to a romantic interpretation of the past where elements of the cottage or Victorian style are preserved as long as they do not interfere with the comforts of twentieth-century living. Original fireplaces are restored, but used to supplement central heating; mouldings and architraves are repaired but painted with white gloss paint; oil or gas lamps are wired for electricity. Only the New Georgians, dedicated to renovating their Georgian homes (they even wear the dress of the period) are willing to renounce modern conveniences for authenticity!

As with fashions in dress, trends in furnishing and design follow each other so fast that it's often hard to keep pace. Here's a look at a few.

Memphis is a decorating style with a fifties air, emphasizing angles and combining black with turquoise, coral, lemon and grey. Colours are set out in blocks, spattered or streaked. It's a bright, colourful style which owes a lot to the 1951 Festival of Britain (though it's actually Italian), with tables and chairs with black metal legs and brightly coloured upholstery, busy abstract designs and contrasting plain and patterned pottery.

Memphis is colourful and fun, but as it is likely to

date it is best to choose long-life items such as furniture in charcoal or black and reserve the brightest colour combinations for textiles or paint.

Finishing touches

Doors can be painted different bright colours to contrast with each other and the walls.

Windows may have fine Venetian blinds in black, bright colours, or mirror effect.

Walls are painted plain grey, blue, lemon or coral, or striped or spattered.

Floors are covered in vinyl or profile-design tiles, spattered or grid-effect sheet flooring or close-pile fitted (wall-to-wall) carpet.

Accessories may be china and furniture in a mixture of bright colours emphasized by black.

Neo-classicism means copying the classical style of Greek or Roman temples, with a nod towards the late Georgian style which was also influenced by these cultures.

Not very apt for today's homes, you may think – but if you've ever considered draping fabric over a curtain pole, allowing full-length curtains to sweep the floor, or putting a vase on a plinth or pedestal, you've been influenced by neo-classicism! Other elements include tiled floors, chairs swathed in fabric and beautiful marble mantelpieces. Textures are smooth and often shiny, there's little pattern in evidence, and the emphasis is on neutrals, especially grey, black and white.

Finishing touches

Doors are panelled, often painted white.

Windows may be draped in sheer fabric (e.g. cheesecloth).

Walls may be sponged or dragged in two closely related colours.

Floors could feature marble effect tiles.

Accessories could be plinths bearing busts or large vases, classical fireplaces in marble or slate, tall mirrors and low couches.

Japanese-inspired rooms are starkly furnished to emphasize the horizontal. Seating, tables and storage are low because the Japanese sit and sleep nearer floor level than we do in the West. Accessories are few and carefully arranged, often in asym-

This draped interior demonstrates the recent enthusiasm for neo-classicism. Note especially the carefully chosen furniture and fireplace, the plinths, bare floor and walls and swathes of filmy fabric.

This sparsely furnished bedroom contains key elements of the Oriental style. A wood and paper screen covers the window, the headboard is painted lacquer red and other colours are confined to black, white and grey.

metric styles which derive from the traditional Japanese art of flower arranging. Most of the shapes will be rectangular (though simple curves are also part of this style) and colours are confined to tones of black, white, red, yellow and blue plus a little grey. There's a marked absence of pattern, and where it is found, the motifs are, more often than not, likely to be abstract.

The purity of this style is its main attraction and it has inspired many recent room settings and furnishing trends. The futon (a Japanese-inspired sofabed) is now readily available and its influence is seen in more conventional upholstery with duvet-style (continental quilt-style) cushions and removable covers. Choose this style to make the most of space in a small modern house or apartment but remember that it doesn't lend itself to cosy clutter. It's basically 'minimalist' – which means that only what's essential for comfort or effect is included.

Finishing touches
Doors should merge with the walls.
Windows may have white pleated blinds.
Walls should be white, cool pastel or grey.
Floors are covered in plain sheet flooring or tiles or plain fitted (wall-to-wall) carpet.
Accessories could be screens, futons or floor cushions in primary colours, simple, sculptural vases and china, and low tables.

High-tech makes use of industrial materials and office furniture in a domestic environment, transforming utilitarian metal and rubber by painting and dyeing them bright primary colours.

The scaffolding and hospital beds which were fashionable at the height of high tech are no longer much in evidence, but their influence can be seen in the steel shelving, clamp lights, and industrial-style flooring on sale. They are ideal for kitchens, bathrooms and playrooms, even if you prefer a more traditional style for the living room and bedroom. Remember that it's still possible to buy steel lockers and shelf systems from office supplies' stores and paint them with gloss or enamel paint to achieve a budget-price high-tech look.

Finishing touches
Doors should have functional steel door furniture.
Windows may have Venetian or plain roller blinds.
Walls should be painted in silk (semigloss) finish emulsion (latex).
Floors may be covered in profile-design or grid-patterned sheet flooring or needlepunch carpeting.
Accessories could be clamp lights and Anglepoise lamps, industrial-style shelving, grid storage, metal furniture and appliances and tractor stools.

Romantic revival styles see the twentieth century in retreat. The look is prompted by nostalgia for the comfort and security associated with the past but, because no one is prepared to throw away the vacuum cleaner or refrigerator, this style combines the elements of the cottage and Victorian styles most suited to modern living.

Choose textile designs which are copied from Victorian originals but recoloured in bright or pastel tones, and furniture made from natural wood. Kitchen units (cabinets) should have at least a veneer of pine, oak or mahogany, topped by a quarry-tiled or hardwood worktop. Floorboards may be sanded and sealed or covered with sisal or plain carpet. Cover upholstery with floral loose covers and use traditional china and prints for decoration. Think Laura Ashley and you're there.

Finishing touches
Doors should be stripped pine or painted with eggshell (or semigloss) finish.
Windows are covered with floral print curtains, lace panels, or festoon blinds.
Walls have floral wallpapers or emulsion (latex) paint. Patterns may be combined, using a dado.

Floors are stripped and sanded, with rugs. *Accessories* could be traditional china in display cabinets or shelf units, prints, baskets, flowering plants and floral table linen.

YOUR OWN HOME

What most of us end up with, however, is the 'eclectic' style influenced by a variety of fashions. As few of us want to live in a museum piece or a modern showcase, we try to translate the looks we like into practical and comfortable homes. Deliberately mixing styles also works well if it is carried out sensitively, using one or two pieces to contrast with the prevailing look. A piece of steel furniture in a Victorian setting or an example of Victorian Gothic in a simple modern one can give great impact.

Prefer something softer? This room combines floral curtains with ribbon tie-backs, a traditional sofa, wicker baskets and a patchwork centrepiece in fashionable colours to create a romantic revival setting.

CHAPTER 2

Assessing your needs

What sort of a person are you and what are your likes and dislikes? Equally important, do you have a large family, are you half of a couple or do you live alone? How much time do you spend at home, and how much money do you want to spend on it? Do you work at home or have any absorbing hobbies? Are you disabled in any way? Do you keep pets – and if so, is the pet a St Bernard or a Siamese cat?

These questions should not only be considered before you redecorate or refurnish. They are also worth asking when you want to modify an existing scheme (possibly one you've inherited) to suit your lifestyle. It's important to take them into account or you may find that the rooms on which you have spent so much time and money either become shabby because the furnishings can't withstand the impact of family life, or uncomfortable because you are forcing yourself to adapt to the scheme instead of vice versa. Here are the points to bear in mind.

CHOOSE YOUR STYLE

Look through the checklist of styles in the previous chapter and note those which appeal to you. Read home interest and design magazines, cutting out any pictures you particularly like. You'll probably find that there's a common denominator for each room. The living room may always be decorated in warm colours, or have books on show, for example; the bedroom may always be carpeted, or the kitchen units (cabinets) white. Sort your cuttings and notes into appropriate areas (as in the room-by-room analysis below) and try to define the looks you want. It's generally better to select a scheme you like and then modify it rather than be guided by practical or aesthetic considerations alone. There's no point in choosing hard-wearing or high-fashion furnishings if you don't feel at home with them. If a style, colour or design makes you feel uncomfortable or depressed avoid it, however fashionable, cheap or practical it may be.

Now decide what needs to be done. If the rooms you have already furnished are satisfactory you may simply want to add accessories or to alter the emphasis. You may want a temporary transformation because you can't afford a complete overhaul, or because other rooms take priority. Or you may want to change the room completely and begin your room scheme all over again.

Next make a plan of each room, indicating north. Paste it to a piece of cardboard large enough to take fabric snippets of all the soft furnishings and upholstery you must keep and swatches of the paint colours, borders or fabrics you want to add. Decorators call this a 'colour board' and it's an invaluable at-a-glance guide to what does, and does not, go! View it in artificial and natural light because tungsten, fluorescent and daylight can radically affect colour, and remember that it will not give any impression of scale. Borrow a large sample of carpet, wall covering or curtain fabric from the retailer (who will usually agree if you offer a deposit) so that you can gauge the effect of a large pattern, and mark on the plan the size and location of any pieces of furniture you intend to buy.

Finally, make a note of which tasks, and rooms, should be tackled first. Although it can be more satisfying to finish one room at a time, it's often not possible if you need to carry out major work like rewiring or installing central heating. Not only will this disrupt several rooms at once, it also alters the order in which you tackle redecoration. Bear in mind, too, your future plans. There's little point in papering the living room if you want to change the windows next year, or installing units (cabinets) in a kitchen you are planning to extend before long.

FAMILY MATTERS

The age and number of people in the house should have a profound influence on your choice of furnishings. If you have three young children, for example, it's simply not worth choosing a pale living room carpet if you have to ban the family from using the french doors or spend your time shouting at the kids to change into slippers. As it's equally irritating if the carpet looks dirty within days of shampooing, the answer is to choose a deeper colour for the carpet and leave pale carpets to singles, couples and those in high-rise apartments; you can always use a pastel-coloured paint or washable wall covering on the walls.

Think long-term. If you're choosing furnishings to last the next 10 years, consider the changes that may affect your lifestyle. If you intend to move house, invest in furniture and accessories which will travel with you, keep built-in furniture to a minimum and choose budget-price floor and window co-

A room of your own is essential if you run a business from home. This home office for two shows how to make the most of space by using floor-to-ceiling box units for storing papers and files, and lengths of worktop for desk space between.

verings as these are items which rarely adapt to the size and shape of new rooms. If you want to have children, consider the impact of a toddler on your upholstery and wallcoverings. You'll need wipe-clean surfaces which won't be ruined by finger-marks – or a felt tip pen! If, on the other hand, you expect children to leave home within the next few years you can afford to splash out on previously impractical colours and designs and you may not

need to replace a jumbo-size freezer or washing machine with an identical model. Teenagers will need privacy for entertaining friends and doing homework, so turn their bedrooms into bedsits (studios). The same applies if you expect to have an elderly relative coming to live with you. Think about allocating a bedroom (downstairs if possible) and adding an extra lavatory.

Always tell retailers the size of your family when

you shop for furnishings and don't assume they are being personal if they ask you about your circumstances! Only by taking these into account can staff help you make an informed choice about the durability of carpets and upholstery fabrics or the practicality of colours.

TIME AND MONEY

If you're at home all day you may have different decorating priorities from someone who goes out to work. If small children keep you at home, you may want to concentrate on combining the kitchen with a safe play area, or making a family room. If you study at home, you'll want to provide an area or room where you can work in peace. If you have retired, you may want to ensure that the living room looks attractive morning and noon as well as night, and that it's warm and cheap to heat.

Which brings us to money. Few people can afford to refurnish or decorate a house in weeks or even months. It may take years, in which case it is a good idea to make a long-term plan of work, tackling priority areas like the bathroom, kitchen or living room first. If money is tight, you will need to plan carefully because you can't afford to discard your mistakes. Try to buy good quality in the case of items which receive the most wear, such as upholstery and furniture; choose hard-wearing carpet and a comfortable bed, and economize on wall coverings, curtains, bedlinen and accessories. Use cheap materials lavishly rather than expensive ones meanly, substituting cheesecloth for cotton satin and sheet flooring for carpet, for example. Indulge in a few decorating 'treats' like a few pieces of handmade crystal or an original painting, an antique table or a clock to cheer you up and give an expensive air to the scheme. But because an expensive storage unit may make a cheap dining table look shoddy, and sumptuous upholstery can look totally out of place on sheet vinyl, be sure to mix the quality of larger furnishings with care.

WORK AND LEISURE

If you work at home or have a time-consuming hobby you'll need to set aside an appropriate area. First decide whether you need an office or a workshop. An office, study or sewing room can be created in a spare bedroom or a corner of the living room if necessary – though remember that you will not be able to shut yourself away from the family, and the television, unless you have a room of your own. Messy pursuits are best kept to a workshop with a separate entrance to avoid dirt or shavings being walked through the house. If this is impossible, consider converting a utility room or basement if you have one or improving the garage or garden shed. (Remember that you'll need both heat and light.) Next make a list of the equipment you use – a computer or sewing machine, for example. Make sure you have sufficient electric sockets in the right place and work out the amount of storage you require. Will a small filing cabinet be sufficient or do you need shelves for reference books or cupboards for fabric? Then design a workstation, where everything you use regularly is close to hand. A desk is not always ideal; take a tip from kitchen planners and consider a worktop with shelves above and cupboards to one side which gives you plenty of room to spread and store your work. Finally, make sure you have a comfortable chair which supports the small of your back (swivel chairs are useful as they extend your reach) and adequate lighting (see page 36).

HEALTHY LIVING

Anyone who is wheelchair-bound knows the importance of wide doorways, slopes in place of steps, stair lifts and rails by the bed and toilet. But disability isn't confined to those who are obviously handicapped. If a member of the family has asthma or eczema, for example, you should choose polyester in place of feather-filled pillows and duvets (comforters), acrylic rather than woollen blankets, and mattresses and upholstery made with foam rather than horse hair. In addition, there are the measures everyone needs to take to ensure safety in the home. Choose non-slip flooring for bathrooms and kitchens, keep knives in a special block or on a rack, provide adequate lighting on stairs, and never overload sockets. Remember that textured flooring may trap dirt – and the kitchen and bathroom are two areas which it is vital to keep clean for the sake of your health. If you are middle-aged, plan for the time when you may no longer be as agile as you are now. Choose high-back upholstery which is not too close to the ground or adjustable reclining chairs and replace mats or rugs with fitted (wall-to-wall) carpet when the time comes for refurbishing.

PET SCHEMES

Dogs and cats can make even greater demands on your furnishings than children. In wet weather all dogs have muddy paws and you will need sheet flooring or dark, close-pile carpet in the hall as well as a washable floor in the kitchen to minimize the

problem. It's wise to keep the dog off your sofas or give him a special chair to spare your upholstery. Boisterous dogs will knock over china ornaments unless these are displayed at a high level and as most dogs shed hair, you'll need to avoid very dark or very pale carpets and to buy a vacuum cleaner with a beater to pick up it up. Remember that puppies chew almost anything, especially when bored, so try to protect your skirtings (baseboards), cupboards and upholstery.

Cats cause different problems. The worst damage they inflict is by sharpening their claws so give your cat a scratching pole if you don't want it to use your furniture. Take special care when choosing loop-pile carpets because cats' claws may catch in them and fray the fibres.

Gracious living is not incompatible with children and pets, though it's certainly easier to be design-conscious if you have only yourself to consider. Families and pet-owners should choose materials and furnishings with care and must be prepared to spend more on furnishings than singles and couples because the most durable materials are usually the best, and most expensive, quality. It's also a policy which anyone who intends to stay in the same house and who wants their furnishings to go on looking good should follow. But because life is something that happens while you're busy making plans, many of us will be caught on the hop by a change of income (welcome or unwelcome), an unexpected move or even an unexpected arrival. That's why the following pages contain ideas for adapting schemes which no longer suit your needs as well as points to consider when furnishing, or refurnishing, your home.

CHAPTER 3

Planning your home

Every home has individual features which will affect the colour scheme and room plan. A large, light living room adapts to a greater number of schemes than one that's small and dark, for example, while a kitchen/dining room needs to be planned in a different way to a kitchen reserved for food preparation alone. Whatever the size and style of your home, the rooms will fall into one of the following categories. Here are some general points to consider when redecorating a room, plus some instant solutions to change a scheme you dislike.

ROUTEWAYS

That's the best description for the hall, stairs and landing, which intersect the house. Though the hall has dwindled in significance since medieval times when it was the most important room in the manor, it is still important because it takes the brunt of the dirt and weather brought in from outside. We gain access to every other room via the hall, stairs and landing, and speed and safety are as important in the traffic ways inside the home as they are outside it. Both need to be kept clear of obstructions, clad with hard-wearing and non-slip surfaces and equipped with good, clear lighting.

Layout needs to be well planned for safety. Clear the way in a narrow hall by using wall rather than floor-mounted storage. Don't be tempted to place chests or tables in the centre of a square hall to fill up space; keep furniture to the sides to prevent aggravation when passing through.

Paint should be washable and hard-wearing. The most durable paints are solvent-based (also called oil-based or alkyd in the US), and a mid-sheen finish like eggshell (or semigloss) on both walls and woodwork will wipe clean and resist knocks from prams (strollers) and shopping bags. If you prefer emulsion (latex) for walls teamed with gloss for woodwork, consider a silk (semigloss) finish which can be cleaned easily and reflects the light. Avoid matt-finish emulsion (flat-finish latex) paint if you have children who leave sticky fingermarks as it becomes shiny if constantly rubbed clean. Choose a receding colour like grey, cool beige or azure to increase the impression of space and paint doors to blend with the walls; strong colour should be confined to accents like a brightly painted coat-stand. In a large hall, opt for deep, rich colours which have an enclosing effect, offset by white.

Wallcoverings should be vinyl or coated with a wipe-clean finish. They vary in washability from scrubbable to wipeable. Look for the symbols in the sample book or on the reverse of the roll which indicate whether the wallpaper is washable. A small pattern makes the most of a cramped hall or cottage landing and random designs obscure uneven walls, but avoid fussy or multi-coloured patterns. Large florals may look out of place even in a grand hall – look for formal or geometric designs instead. Woodchip and relief wallcoverings may be used as a base for paint as they conceal rough plaster, but remember that over-painted wallpaper is the most difficult to strip!

Flooring must conceal dirt and withstand the abrasion it causes. You don't *have* to carpet the hall. Sheet or cushioned vinyls provide a resilient, washable surface, while ceramic or quarry tiles are both hard-wearing and easy to clean. Absorbent materials, like cork and wood, are best sealed with at least three coats of polyurethane varnish to repel damp. You need not seal wood if you are prepared to settle for a matt (flat) finish, but don't try to polish wood floors to a high shine in the hall unless carpet is strategically placed to cover areas of greatest wear. Smooth floorings should be swept and damp-mopped when needed. Polishing is unnecessary, but what is essential is to wipe away wet patches as soon as they occur to prevent falls.

The carpet you choose for routeways in a two-storey house should be recommended for use on stairs, which exact more wear from carpet than any other area. Most foam-backed carpets are unsuitable, as are long-pile carpets which tend to 'grin' on the risers. Look for a brand suitable for heavy domestic use (often denoted by a pictorial representation of a hall and stairs on the carpet sample). Suitable fibres include acrylic, third-generation nylon, high-grade polyester, pure wool (very expensive) and the traditional blend of 80 per cent wool and 20 per cent nylon. Plain carpet makes the most of space but shows the dirt more than patterned. Compromise with a small geometric design if your hall receives heavy wear, or choose a deep-colour plain carpet with a resilient twist pile. Always add door mats to take the brunt of the dirt.

Finishing touches

Window coverings are not essential unless the hall is overlooked, and are best omitted if the window is an attractive architectural feature. Where necessary, choose a material which blends with the walls (unless the window is large) as small contrasting curtains may look busy and spoil the proportions of the hall. Choose a patterned fabric which co-ordinates with the wallpaper or a plain material with a contrasting trim – or opt for roller, Roman or festoon blinds (see page 46).

Furniture should never obstruct a passageway – which means that it's best kept to a minimum in the average hall. You will need storage for coats and boots (a cupboard or closet is the best solution as hooks and racks look untidy) and a seat plus chest or table for the telephone if yours is sited here. Keep the floor completely clear of furniture if you want to prevent the hall from becoming a dumping ground for bits and pieces on their way up or down stairs.

Lighting should be designed for safety rather than atmosphere, illuminating possible hazards like a turn in the stairs. Fit multiple or track-mounted spotlights to supplement background lighting and add a dimmer if you have children or elderly relatives who are liable to get up at night.

Mirrors can be used to reflect natural light, often limited in routeways, as well as to check your appearance before you answer the door. Choose a mirror that's in keeping with the style of your house (a gilt-framed pier mirror for a period home, a simply framed panel for a modern one, for example). Place full-length mirrors with care, avoiding areas where children may run into them or where guests may be surprised by the sight of an approaching figure!

This welcoming hall is plainly and practically decorated with white painted walls, coir matting and the minimum of furniture. The rug, carved chair and turned legs of the hall table add interest while a floor vase serves as an umbrella stand.

FACESAVERS

● Exploit the potential of a square hall by adding a bureau where papers can be shut away if there is no room for a separate study elsewhere, or, if you have no dining room, a dining table which can be pushed against the wall when not in use.

● A ceiling that's too high can be painted a deep shade. Continue the colour down to the picture rail, if there is one, to emphasize the effect.

● A dado allows you to combine a pretty but impractical wallcovering with a washable or dark coloured paint finish or companion paper lower down and makes it possible to remove damaged wallpaper at the base of the wall without having to strip the entire area.

● Add a new-style carpet runner to hide carpet that has seen better days or is in a pattern or colour you dislike. A neutral coir (coconut fibre) runner with a striped border and matching doormat is chic; choose one with bound ends which won't fray and latex (rubber) backing which is more practical and won't slip.

● Place a mirror opposite a window to reflect the light. Be careful not to place it at the end of a hallway or staircase, though, or it could possibly confuse visitors.

Make the most of space by choosing light-reflecting colours like the white walls and tiled floor of this narrow hall, continued into the room beyond for maximum effect. The understairs space has been adapted to form an unusual bookcase.

Pictures break up the long stretches of wall. Combine shapes and sizes to form groups along the stairs or a wall, but make sure the frames and styles are compatible. Use decorative plates to add interest and consider a key plate by the front door to save the usual frantic search.

WORK AREAS

The kitchen is the most important work room in the house, often combining the functions of dining room or laundry room and sometimes playroom too.

Layout should include a 'work triangle' linking cooker (stove), sink, refrigerator and food preparation area, joined if possible by a continuous sweep of worktop. The work triangle should not be too large or you will waste energy – 6½ ft (2 m) between each area is about right. In most rooms this is not a problem, but if you have a very large kitchen you should consider adding an island unit to make the equipment more accessible. Remember that the sink, dishwasher and washing machine should be sited against or next to an outside wall to avoid long and unsightly pipe runs.

Most kitchens fall into four basic categories. *U-shaped* kitchens have units (cabinets) on three sides. They are the easiest to work in, but limited to kitchens with only one entrance unless there is space to fit a peninsula unit to form a third side.

L-shaped kitchens have units (cabinets) on two sides. This makes effective use of many kitchens with two entrances.

In-line or one-wall kitchens have units (cabinets) ranged along one wall, the best solution for narrow, corridor-like rooms.

Galley kitchens have units (cabinets) along two walls; many narrow kitchens with two entrances have this arrangement. Ideally the sink and cooker (stove) should be along the same wall to avoid the risk of accidents.

Other safety measures to observe include siting the cooker (stove) away from doors and windows (because draughts may extinguish or fan a flame), fitting top units (overhead cabinets) where there are only cupboards or worktop (counter) beneath and storing knives and cleaning materials at a high level if you have small children. In addition you will need adequate electric points (outlets) and clear 'task' lighting.

Paint should be wipeable and steam-resistant. Solvent-based mid-sheen paint like eggshell (or alkyd semigloss) withstands condensation best but if this is not a problem you can also consider silk or satin emulsion (semigloss latex) which wipes clean. This is not recommended for very steamy kitchens, however, because sheen-finish emulsion (semigloss latex) tends to streak. Modern kitchens often do not have a constant source of heat and may be chilly when the cooker (stove) is not in use, so you may prefer to go for lively tints of primrose and pink which work surprisingly well. Bold primary colours look attractive used to offset white or contrasting coloured units (cabinets), while soft shades and leaf green suit kitchens with stained or natural wood.

Wallcoverings should be washable. Look at vinyl wallcoverings, coated wallpaper and, of course, tiles, which form an impermeable splashback behind worktop and appliances. Patterned wallcoverings which have companion fabrics, tiles or table linen are especially useful in a kitchen/dining room where they help to furnish and co-ordinate the room.

Flooring must be waterproof and easy to clean. Although ceramic and quarry tiles are attractive and durable, they may become slippery when wet and are cold and hard on the feet. Vinyl-coated cork and cushioned vinyl flooring are warm and resilient.

Many sheet floorings are now available in 6 ft 6 in, 9 ft 9 in and 13 ft (2, 3 and 4m) widths to suit most kitchens, but you will find vinyl tiles easier to lay in awkwardly shaped rooms.

Finishing touches

Window coverings should be practical. Blinds (roller or Roman) look neat, stay clear of the worktop and can be chosen to co-ordinate or contrast with furnishings. Short curtains with a wooden pelmet look charming in cottagey kitchens and café curtains, which obscure the bottom of the window for privacy but let in light at the top, are ideal if the kitchen can be peered into from outside. Use a roller blind which co-ordinates with the kitchen colour scheme to cover shelves in a utility room, hiding laundry, washing powder and cleaning materials.

Unit (cabinets) can be painted, stained or stencilled to suit a change of scheme. It's possible to paint laminate with gloss or enamel, provided it is sanded with fine silicone carbide paper before and between coats. Solid wood and veneer units (cabinets) can be stained and finished with clear varnish or coloured and coated in one using a tinted product. Dragging, stippling or stencilling the doors (see page 61) will add visual interest and gives a touch of individual style at very little cost.

Utensils can be decorative as well as functional. Fit a grid storage rack in a modern kitchen, butchers' hooks, baskets or curtain poles in a traditional one and suspend ladles, sieves and jugs from them. Decorate the walls with hanging plates and display attractive bowls and saucepans on cupboards or shelves, instead of hiding them away.

Lighting should illuminate work surfaces so you'll need task lighting provided by lights beneath wall cupboards, spotlights or downlighters, as well as general light.

KITCHEN PLANS

1 An in-line or one-wall kitchen has units (cabinets), sink, cooker (stove) and refrigerator along one wall.
2 The galley kitchen ranges units (cabinets) along two walls.
3 L-shaped kitchens make use of two walls.
4 The U-shaped kitchen has units (cabinets) on three sides.

Units made from old pine are the ideal choice for a country cottage. Team them with a pine table and shelves and crowd the walls with prints, plates and dried flowers and herbs for a traditional look.

FACESAVERS
• Adapt an inefficient layout by adding a butcher block table or gourmet trolley (cart) to provide a mobile food preparation area.
• Can't afford a new built-in kitchen? Fit a length of worktop (countertop) to cover base cupboards and appliances and paint storage, walls and pipes one strong colour to give a sense of unity.
• It's possible to tile over existing tiles if the originals are in good condition and sealed with plaster primer. The double thickness at the top can be concealed with wooden moulding painted or stained to co-ordinate.
• Choose new flooring with care if you don't want to remove or screed over an existing floor. Cushioned vinyl can be laid over most existing hard floors: look for the 'lay flat' variety which only needs adhesive at doorways and under heavy moveable appliances like the cooker (stove) and washing machine.
• Change the handles on kitchen units (cabinets) to give them a brand new look.

Above: White plus a primary accent makes a crisp modern scheme. Here adaptable white units (cabinets) are finished with yellow handles, a colour repeated by the kitchen plastics and the brightly painted beam.

Far right: This small sitting room has a soft colour scheme and every detail has been carefully chosen. Furniture is kept to the sides of the room and storage is built in to increase the sense of space. The pale rug, quilt and drapes reflect the light.

LIVING AREAS

These are the 'public' rooms of the house, where the family meet and friends are entertained. They may also have to cater for a variety of specialized interests like playing or listening to music, studying or sewing. As you are likely to spend a lot of time there, it is worthwhile giving them some careful thought and attention.

Layout needs careful planning, as the living room often doubles as a dining room, playroom or hall.

Living rooms should have a focal point. It needn't be a fireplace, though this can look attractive filled with green plants in summer as well as when it's in use, but it shouldn't be the television, which is best absorbed into a cupboard or storage unit. A room with a view should take advantage of the outlook by grouping the seating by the window, while a wall covered with pictures, or a coffee table with a few selected ornaments, will also attract the eye. Arrange seating in conversational groups, with sofas opposite or at right angles to each other and occasional tables in front or to one side to take care of drinks or books.

Dining rooms need a serving table as well as a central one. This can be a sideboard with storage for china beneath, a console table or a shelf. If the dining room is some distance from the kitchen, add a hot tray so that food doesn't cool down or use a trolley (cart) unless there are changes in level or thick carpet to negotiate. Make sure that the size of the table suits that of the room and remember that

you will need a minimum of 30 inches (80 cm) space round the table to allow for access and comfortable seating. A rectangular dining table makes the best use of space in most rooms and can be pushed against the wall for everyday use but round or oval tables can seat more people and are better for 'help yourself' suppers – a long rectangular table is difficult to manœuvre around and really requires waitress service!

Living/dining rooms and other multi-purpose rooms should be arranged in two (or more) separate areas united by the colour scheme and furnishing style. Take care to keep traffic ways clear and make positive use of them to define the different areas. In many rooms the living and dining areas are clearly marked out by a hatch (hutch) at the dining end or a fireplace in the sitting area. In larger or older homes or converted apartments you may have more choice. If you find that you're not using a certain room, or part of a room, regularly, consider putting it to another use. It may suit your lifestyle better to have a small living room and a large work room/dining room, or to turn the dining room into a playroom, study or bedsit (studio apartment) and eat in the kitchen.

Paint doesn't need to be as hard-wearing as in the kitchen or hall so opt for matt-finish emulsion (flat-finish latex paint) for a velvety look or silk (semigloss) finish to reflect light and to emphasize the texture of relief wall coverings. Eggshell (or alkyd semigloss) is the best choice if you want to try your hand at a paint treatment like sponging or ragging, or if you want an all-surface paint to cover both walls and woodwork. Soft colours which create a restful background for various activities suit most living rooms but dining rooms can afford to look dramatic. Choose colours to set the scene. A formal dining room which is used for dinner parties calls for a rich, elegant scheme in a deep shade like burgundy, ochre or indigo. A dining room that's used for family meals or lunches needs a lighter touch, using colours like peach, cream or grey.

Wall coverings should follow the same rules. Choose designs which are easy to live with for living and living/dining rooms, defining the dining area with a co-ordinating border if required, and reserve more demanding designs for a separate dining room. Look for vinyl or washable wallpaper for a family living or dining room and always buy one more roll than you need so that an accident doesn't become a disaster and you are sure you have a private standby in exactly the right shade.

This pale and interesting sitting room features upholstery and blinds in a delicate version of the popular ikat style. The window coverings are fastened diagonally to emphasize the chevron design.

Flooring for living rooms means some form of carpet to add softness and warmth. It needn't be fitted: abstract pattern, long-pile Rya or Flokati rugs, Chinese, Indian or Oriental carpets, dhurries or Wilton squares all look sumptuous over polished boards or tiles. If you opt for fitted (wall-to-wall) carpet choose one for general or heavy domestic use and remember that plain carpet makes the most of space. If you want to add pattern, consider a bordered carpet to add a designer touch to a regularly shaped room. Where plain carpets are concerned, velvet (or velour) pile looks elegant but shows foot-

marks. If you dislike its characteristic 'shadowing' choose a crush-resistant twist pile instead. Think carefully before you carpet a dining room. Soft flooring muffles the sound of scraping chairs and adds a sense of luxury but demands more care than a smooth floor which is easily cleaned. If your heart is set on a carpeted dining room, however, remember that a pattern can help to obscure marks and dark colours are more practical than pale.

Finishing touches

Window coverings are important in living and dining

FACESAVERS

● Move your furniture to suit the season if space allows, grouping seating by the garden window in summer and round the fireplace in winter.
● Modify dingy paintwork by rubbing a wax crayon over skirtings (baseboards) and door frames to co-ordinate with the walls. This gives an attractive colour-rubbed effect.
● Add a wallpaper frieze to replace a missing picture rail or add interest to plain walls – very effective if it co-ordinates with the fabric used for cushions or curtains.

● Use a large dhurry in colours which co-ordinate with your scheme to cover a worn fitted (wall-to-wall) carpet or one that's the wrong colour. Fit Velcro or anti-creep fibre on the back to stop it moving. For safety, never place rugs at doorways where people could easily trip over them or on polished floors.
● If the living room lighting is inadequate, fit extra flex (cord) to a pendant light and attach with a hook in the ceiling so that it centres over a low table. Supplement it with uplighters and table lamps.

rooms, which usually contain the largest windows in the house. Choose a fabric in keeping with the style of your house and furnishings. Curtains or drapes should normally be to the floor, to the sill or to the height of the radiator if this is immediately beneath the window. If you want full-length curtains (drapes) here, fit a festoon or roller blind to cover the window and add side curtains for show so that you don't exclude the heat. If more than half the wall contains window, it's often a good idea to curtain the entire wall to add to the sense of space. You can afford to use a more dramatic pattern for curtains than wallpaper as the folds of the fabric soften the effect. Don't neglect the heading; there's a wide choice of styles from pelmets (valances) and pleated headings to curtain poles or elaborate swags and tails (see page 46). In a small room choose plain fabric, curtains which match the wallpaper or small designs on a pale ground to make the most of space. Large rooms and windows can take designs on a grand scale and tiny prints may look out of place; borrow a sample length from your retailer before you decide.

Furniture should be considered for its contribution to the colour scheme as well as for comfort and style. Plain upholstery with contrast piping looks especially smart and small geometric designs can be used to offset plain furnishings without clashing with other patterns. Two sofas are often better value for money (and more stylish) than the conventional three-piece suite (set) and one or two feature chairs – a bentwood rocker, a wingback chair, a modern chaise longue or a button-backed chair, for example – help to vary the style, height and shape of the seating group. Storage and tables should be in keeping with your choice of style. Select pieces with a similar degree of formality. They needn't match, but remember that hardwoods and softwoods (rosewood and pine, for example) rarely mix well.

Cushions can add co-ordination. Use remnants of curtain fabric to cover them and choose additional cushions in a colour which relates.

Fireplaces should be in keeping with the style and period of the room. Consider opening up a disused fireplace and replace inappropriate types with a restored or reproduction model – marble, carved oak or pine for an eighteenth-century home, cast iron for a Victorian room or a modern classic.

Pictures and ornaments are important elements of decoration in the living room. Concentrate them in a specific area for best effect; dotting them around the room diminishes their impact.

A neutral scheme based on white, offset by the beige carpet and black table, makes a virtue of simplicity in this budget living room Yellow flowers and luxuriant greenery add living colour.

Lighting has to perform more roles in the living room than in any other. Use pools of light from downlighters, uplighters or table lamps to create atmosphere, spotlights and picture lights to emphasize special architectural features and collections or displays and wall or desk lights for reading. Don't use a pendant light for general lighting; save it for use low down over a dining or occasional table where it will cast a concentrated beam.

PRIVATE PLACES
Bedrooms and bathrooms should be a retreat where you can shut yourself away – temporarily – from family responsibilities and cares. Choose schemes which relax or stimulate as you prefer; after all, you've only yourself (or selves) to please in these particular rooms.

Layout in bedrooms and bathrooms, which are often small, means you should allow sufficient 'activity' space so that you can reach high cupboards, open drawers and use the bath and basin in comfort. A wardrobe or closet should be large enough to accommodate a coat or a long dress. It should measure at least 22 inches (55 cm) in depth with a hanging rail between 60 and 70 inches (152 and 177 cm) high and a top shelf no more than 72 inches (182 cm) high so that it can be reached by a woman of average height. Beware of top cupboards with doors which open upwards, leaving you to support them with one hand while you search around with the other, and opt for drawers rather than shelves for flimsy items like shirts and slips which are difficult to stack. If you want a storage divan (platform bed),

Blue, celadon and white create an appropriately restful bedroom scheme. Full-length curtains (drapes) give importance to the setting while the blue dado defines the bed. The white counterpane provides a crisp contrast.

look for one with drawers which won't be impeded by bedside cupboards, or choose wall-mounted shelves rather than bedside tables. Ergonomics are equally important in the bathroom. If the fixtures are along the same wall, allow 16 inches (40 cm) from the centre of a bidet, basin or lavatory to the edge of the bath, and 20 inches (50 cm) to an end wall or shower cabinet. Leave 32 inches (80 cm) clear in front of a bidet and lavatory, 40 inches (1 m) in front of a bath or washbasin.

Paint needs to resist condensation in the bathroom, so choose eggshell (semigloss latex) if this is a problem. Bedrooms receive less wear than any other room so a restful non-reflective matt emulsion (flat latex) is a good choice, except in children's rooms where it's wise to opt for a finish that's easily washed. Children and teenagers often like bright schemes based on primary colours, but adults usually prefer a more soothing choice of scheme. Consider peach, lemon, celadon (grey-green), silver grey or cream, or a deep enclosing shade like midnight blue or damask rose.

Wall coverings should follow the same rules.

You'll need water-resistant materials in the bathroom (where vinyl wallcovering and ceramic tiles are good choices) and a washable finish in children's rooms but you can afford to select delicate papers, patterns and colours for an adult bedroom. You can buy wallpaper, friezes, curtain fabric and bedlinen all designed to go together which gives a fully co-ordinated look. Choose a small sprig-effect or abstract pattern on a pale ground to make the most of space in small bedrooms or bathrooms and paper the ceiling too. An en-suite (master suite) bathroom should co-ordinate with the bedroom. Use matching or co-ordinating curtain fabric, or paint or paper in a co-ordinating shade or pattern.

Flooring need not be hard-wearing but it must be water-resistant for bathroom use. Choose between carpet made from synthetic fibres (nylon or polyester, in bright or pastel colours, are a popular choice), vinyl tiles (easier to lay in most bathrooms than sheet flooring) and cork, which must be vinyl-coated or sealed to resist moisture. Ceramic tiles are smart but slippery; they may even be too heavy to use in large areas above ground level. Remember that tiles and sheet flooring need a rigid sub-floor – only carpet and underlay should be laid directly over floorboards.

Children's bedrooms need floors which are warm and easy to clean. Avoid long-pile carpet which hinders jigsaw puzzles, board games and wheeled toys and go for cord or polypropylene carpet, cushioned vinyl or cork tiles. Carpet is the favourite for adult bedrooms, where a thick Saxony pile adds a sense of luxury. Choose a tone which co-ordinates with the colour scheme and don't be afraid of pastels, especially in nylon or polyester, which are easy to clean, although pure wool has an unbeatable richness of colour. Use the same flooring throughout a bedroom with en-suite (master-suite) bathroom, but keep to synthetic fibres; some lines contain bedroom and bathroom carpet in identical shades.

Finishing touches

Window coverings vary with the room's style but are generally lighter than in living rooms. Blinds are practical in bathrooms: choose between flouncy festoons, sleek Venetian and roller blinds, pleated or Roman blinds. Long drapes look attractive in large or double bedrooms but short ones (to sill length) are more appropriate in tiny rooms. Use dark linings (contrasting lining in a strong colour looks especially smart) or light-resistant blinds in children's rooms to deter the dawn chorus!

Mirrors are essential in both bedrooms and bathrooms, but use them decoratively to reflect the light. Make sure they are in the appropriate place and at the right height.

Plants flourish in humid bathrooms and light bedrooms. Use hanging baskets to add interest to a dull corner or mass plants on shelves or small tables to make a living screen.

Soaps and cosmetics look attractive if chosen with care. Pile soaps into a china dish or basket in the bathroom where they look pretty and scent the air.

Horizontal stripes on the walls and bath panel add width to this tiny bathroom. White bathroom ware helps increase the sense of space while the sealed floor gives warmth and the attractive window frames provide decorative interest.

Put attractive containers and perfume bottles on display, but shut away any unsightly items.

Furniture can be decorative as well as comfortable. Look at corner cupboards, dark wood or stripped pine shelves, wooden towel horses and cane chairs when furnishing the bathroom and add a button-back chair or chaise longue in a co-ordinating colour when furnishing (outfitting) the bedroom. Paint or stain garden chairs or second-hand furniture if you are furnishing on a budget.

Bedlinen can co-ordinate with curtain fabric and wallpaper but if you use a duvet (continental quilt) remember that you'll need two sets of covers to wash and wear. To avoid the expense of buying new, consider making a fitted or quilted bedspread or comforter from curtain fabric or sheets, or opt for plain white, ecru or lace covers.

Lighting should be relaxing. Pendant or wall lights will give sufficient overall light but remember to provide adequate bedside lighting and lights behind or around a mirror for making-up.

FACESAVERS

● A screen (wooden or covered in fabric to match the curtains) can be used to conceal a clothes rail or dressing area.

● Change an unsympathetic colour scheme by sponging off-white eggshell (or semigloss) finish over existing paint. Co-ordinate a child's room by stencilling walls or furniture to repeat a motif on bedlinen or curtains.

● Add interest to cheap built-in wardrobes or closets by creating panels with mouldings and co-ordinating wallpaper.

● Can't afford a carpet? Colour-rub floorboards to blend with the scheme using eggshell finish (or alkyd semigloss) diluted with white spirit.

● Cover an unattractive headboard with an envelope of fabric chosen to co-ordinate with the scheme. Quilt and pipe it for an expensive look.

CHAPTER 4

How to colour scheme

There's a greater choice of colour today than at any other time in history. Colour-fast synthetic dyes have made bright, long-lasting colours a possibility while easy-care finishes and modern appliances have simplified their care. No wonder colour is now the dominant consideration in home decoration – even if a home is furnished in black and white. That's as strong a statement as primary colours and just as difficult to co-ordinate, as you will know if you have ever tried to match different materials in these tones! A single paint system may provide a thousand tints and shades from which to choose and there's increasing interest in co-ordinated furnishings, with fabrics, wallpaper, paint, bedlinen, tiles and accessories designed to go together.

Your schemes will be more flexible, however, if you learn how to use colour independently. It's not simply a matter of flair, because colour scheming is a skill which can be acquired. This does involve learning a little theory, but it's worth knowing how colour works because if you're ever stuck for a shade to provide that perfect finishing touch, you'll be able to assess what you need without going through all the fabric or paint samples in the store.

WHAT IS COLOUR?

Colour is simply a trick of the light. All the colours we see derive from the colours of the rainbow (or light broken up by a prism) which are violet, blue, green, yellow, orange and red. Three of these, red, yellow and blue, are constant and cannot be formed by mixing other hues together. These are commonly known as the primary colours. The others, violet, green and orange, are called secondary colours, because they are made by mixing the primary colours – blue and red for violet, blue and yellow for green and yellow and red for orange.

THE COLOUR WHEEL

Twist the rainbow to form a circle and you create the colour wheel. There are several versions of this, but one of the easiest to understand places the primary colours in the centre, or inner wheel, and the secondary hues beyond. On the rim of the wheel are the tertiary colours, formed by mixing primaries and secondaries together. That gives you intermediate colours like blue/green or yellow/green. Co-lours near to each other on the colour wheel are called related colours because they blend. Those opposite each other are called, confusingly if accurately, complementary colours. Think of them as contrasts rather than companions.

NEUTRALS

The only true neutral is grey, because it is a mixture of the two important 'non-colours', black and white. In practice, however, cream, beige and sometimes brown (actually a form of orange) are also considered to be neutrals because they provide relief from bright colours and harmonize with otherwise incompatible hues.

WARM AND COOL COLOURS

Red, yellow and orange are called warm colours because they are associated with sources of heat – the sun and fire. Blue and green are cool colours because of their relationship with the sea and sky; violet is more ambiguous as it can be mixed with blue to form lavender, a cool colour, or red to form mauve, which is warm. As well as producing sensations of warmth or cold, colours also affect our perception of distance. The warm colours are also called 'advancing' colours because they make objects seem larger and nearer (which is why red is a favourite colour for packaging) while cool tones are 'receding' colours because they appear further away. So what do you use in a small, cold room where you need to increase the sense of space and add warmth or a large, warm one where you want the reverse? The answer is to use a tint of a warm colour or a shade of a cool one (see Types of colour scheme, page 31).

VALUE AND INTENSITY

Value measures light and dark. The colours in the rainbow and the colour wheel are pure colours (also called hues or tones). Add white to a pure colour and you have a tint, or pastel. Mix it with black and you create a shade. You can minimize the effect of an ugly window or fireplace by choosing curtains or paint in the same tonal value as the wall. The effect is increased if you choose the same colour as well, but it works even with contrasting colours.

Intensity describes bright and dull. The impact of colours is blunted by adding a little contrasting co-

lour to a tone, for example to produce burgundy rather than scarlet.

TYPES OF COLOUR SCHEME

The three types of colour scheme are based on the single, related and complementary tones on the colour wheel.

One-colour or monochromatic schemes use a single tone in different shades to add variety. These schemes can be surprisingly difficult to create because you need to take care to keep to different strengths of the same colour and not to blur the impact by using related colours. This may not be important: blue/violet looks very attractive with blue, for example. But it can be crucial if you stray too far so experiment carefully.

Use white or a neutral to point up a one-colour scheme in smaller rooms, accents of a contrasting colour in a large or important one.

Pure tones don't have to be used for accents: terracotta may look more effective than crimson in a green room and apricot prettier than orange in one that's predominantly blue. Because you'll be using a splash of contrasting colour, its effect will be emphasized, so be sure to choose the items it will be used on with great care.

Little things mean a lot. Try contrasting piping on curtain tie-backs, cushions or upholstery to pep up a scheme that's lacking in style, or paint door or cupboard mouldings white or a 'natural' white which contains a hint of contrasting colour to add extra interest to a room scheme.

Bright accents add life to a neutral scheme. These vibrant pink cushions are set against black and white furnishings for maximum impact – but it's not a colour you would choose for the walls.

Related schemes use blends or colours near to each other on the colour wheel. Once again, the scheme is not limited to pure tones, though all those you use should contain the same primary colour. Yellow, orange and orange/yellow are colours which blend, for example, but so do primrose and pale green or pink and mauve.

Choose colours which blend to alter the impact of a scheme. (This is particularly helpful if you are stuck with furnishings in a colour you dislike.) Add primrose-coloured curtains plus cushions or a bedspread to a room with a dark green carpet and mid-green walls, for example, or choose a yellow, green and white pattern for a fresh effect. Add blue/violet trimmed tie-backs to purple curtains and sponge the walls the same colour. Introduce a pink armchair and blind in a room decorated in maroon, and add a pink/beige rug or a dhurry in pink and burgundy.

The colours you add need not be light. Reverse the process if the room is pink by adding details in burgundy – or choose bright colours like pink with orange for a completely different effect!

Complementary schemes use contrasting colours, but rarely at full strength. The opposite of blue is orange, but few of us would want to live in a room decorated in these tones, and the same goes for red and its opposite, green, or yellow and violet. Shift the emphasis to navy and peach, or pink and dark green, however, and you will see how effective complementary schemes using tints and shades can be.

Complementary schemes are not restricted to two colours. You can use three contrasting tones – the three primary colours, sugar almond pastels, or tertiary colours like chartreuse (yellow/green), flame (red/orange) and steel (blue/violet). You can use the colours on either side of the true contrast, or two pairs of contrasting colours.

A careful balance of colour is essential when creating a complementary scheme. Too much of each and the effect will be overpowering, too little and it will be lost. One trick is to choose contrasting colours for two main surfaces and combine them in a pattern on the other. Think of pale coral walls with a leaf-green carpet and coral and green-patterned curtains, for instance, or scarlet units (cabinets), apple white walls and a red and green blind in a kitchen. Primrose walls, a lavender/grey carpet and primrose and lilac curtains and bed linen are ideal for a pretty bedroom.

Use contrasting colours to add drama to a dull scheme. If you've never considered green carpet exciting, paint the woodwork scarlet, add wallpaper which combines red and green on white … and take another look. Create a rich, traditional scheme by adding drapes with a green motif on a wine/red ground, and add an armchair which mingles wine with white in a classic geometric design like houndstooth check or fleur de lys.

TEXTURE

Texture is often the last aspect that's considered when decorating a room – yet its importance should not be overlooked, especially where pattern is absent. Texture not only adds variety to plain furnishings, it also modifies the effect of colour. While rough or matt textures absorb light and appear to add warmth, shiny ones reflect it and create a cooler atmosphere. A colour that's light-absorbing, like olive green, may seem black when used for carpet or velvet upholstery if light is limited, while a colour that's reflective, like white, may look chilly used on shiny surfaces like tiles.

TEXTURE AND PATTERN

Shiny textures emphasize pattern, which is why silk (or semigloss) finish paint is usually recommended for use over relief wall coverings (popular in Britain) to highlight the design. But though matt textures make a design less obvious, remember that matt texture plus pattern plus deep or advancing colour (as on some sculptured pile carpet, chenille curtaining or flock wallpaper) has an enclosing effect.

MIXING TEXTURES

There's no need for vivid colours or pattern in a room where textures contrast – and, conversely, a variety of textures is vital in a room decorated in plain, neutral colours. Think of the difference between a room with walls painted in matt emulsion (flat latex paint) and furnished with needlepunch carpet and closely woven curtains and upholstery, and one with the same walls but a shiny floor partly covered by a deep pile rug, a mirror-effect Venetian blind and tweed or leather upholstery.

Counteract the coldness of a smooth floor by adding a long-pile rug. Heavy woven curtains or wooden or cane blinds will offset silk finish emulsion (silk or semigloss latex paint) or vinyl wallcovering. Add mirrors and glass-topped tables for variety in a room where warm textures predominate. Introduce cane or wood into a kitchen to offset laminate units (cabinets).

Bold colours and shapes can work well together if chosen with care. This leaf design on walls, vase and lampshade contains two complementary colours, coral and green, on a peach ground, co-ordinating with geometric motifs in the same colours. Textural interest is provided by the cool white marble fireplace, complete with shiny, ceramic tiles, dried flowers, and softly draped throw.

Above: Co-ordinated ranges of furnishings make for foolproof colour schemes. Here the chintzy sofa fabric is offset by striped cushions, check curtains (drapes) and paisley print blinds – a combination of fabrics designed to go well together.

Right: Like neutral colours, abstract designs form a restful background to bold patterns or, used alone, create schemes which are easy to live with. Choose stripes, checks or chevrons, or stylized designs based on leaves or flowers.

PATTERN

A quick and virtually foolproof way to colour scheme is to let the professionals do it for you. Take advantage of the expertise that has gone into selecting the colours used in a pattern on wallpaper, fabric or carpet, and use these tones for other furnishings. Extend the theme for complete co-ordination, linking rooms by the use of colour, so that the apricot of the living room is repeated in the blue and apricot frieze in the hall and the blue in the hall is taken up by the cream and navy kitchen. Choose tints rather than bold colours in large areas where you want to reflect light and pick shades for areas subject to wear, like the carpet.

LARGE AND SMALL

Large patterns have the same effect as advancing colours; they reduce the impression of space. In contrast, abstract stippled designs in related colours and delicate sprig patterns on a white ground may, like receding colours, increase the sense of space. The size of the pattern is not the only important factor, because a large pattern in pale, receding colours may blend into the background more than one with small, multi-coloured motifs which will tend to look busy. In addition, a design will stand out more on a flat surface (like wallpaper or carpet) than on a gathered one, which is why co-ordinating ranges usually save bold designs for curtains and provide neater patterns for wallpaper. It's also wise to choose a design which suits the proportions of your room. Though you're unlikely to pick an overwhelmingly large pattern for a small room, don't be tempted to use too small a design in a large one, with the exception of abstract self-coloured designs which imitate texture rather than shape. Remember that most patterns have a repeat. Small random designs are called 'free match' because there's no need to align lengths, but in all other cases you'll need to allow extra wallpaper, fabric or carpet to ensure that you end up with a correct match.

MIXING PATTERNS

Why risk mixing patterns? Because, despite careful colour scheming, there sometimes seems to be too great a divide between plain and patterned areas. Patterned curtains, for example, may have little in common with plain carpet, walls and upholstery, especially if the room is large.

What's needed in these cases is a geometric pattern or an abstract design. These can perform the same roles as a neutral colour, providing a breathing space between the main areas of interest. Choose striped wallpaper to offset chintz curtains and chair covers. Alternatively, you could use a random design which mimics the popular sponged, dragged, stippled or rag-rolled paint treatments – soft effects which give the wall depth as well as interest and bridge the gap between pattern and plain.

Blend patterned and plain furnishings by giving patterned curtains plain tie-backs which match the upholstery or carpet.

Use remnants of curtain fabric and co-ordinating designs for cushions and table covers.

Use a frieze, paper or stencilled, to combine the colours of a plainly furnished room.

PART TWO

THE BASIC INGREDIENTS

Have you stretched your resources to the limit to buy your home and equip it with the basics? Perhaps you're furnishing for the second time around, and determined to do it in style. Or perhaps you've just moved house and need a temporary cover-up. Whatever your circumstances, there's something in this section for you. It includes ideas for choosing your major accessories — lighting, window coverings and floorings — together with tips for using the fashionable borders and drapes which give any home a sense of style.

CHAPTER 5

Bright ideas

Far right: While pools of light create atmosphere, many of the lights in this room have a specific purpose too. Table lamps are placed behind the sofa for reading, a picture light illuminates the painting above and a pendant light is centred above the dining table.

Lighting can give general background light, highlight pictures or ornaments, create atmosphere or provide clear working light – and it's essential for safety. Yet how many homes get by with a single light in the centre of the room, plus bedside lights and a table lamp or two in the living room? Properly designed, artificial lighting can be used decoratively to alter the effect of colour and shift the room's focal point. Don't forget that you can control natural light too, by using mirrors to reflect every bit of daylight and increase its effect, or blinds or shutters to filter it.

TYPES OF LIGHT

Ceiling-mounted lights fall into two distinct categories: first, functional opal glass globes, plastic drums and tubular fluorescent fittings which cast a brighter light. Fit a diffuser to soften the glare of this type of light.
Good for: general light in small rooms
Not for: mood lighting
Second, multiple lights are primarily for decoration. Those which point downwards give direct light, while designs which throw light on to the ceiling give indirect, or reflected, light.
Good for: creating atmosphere and contributing to the room's style

Not for: task lighting or, alone, for general light
Desk lights should be adjustable. They usually direct a clear beam on to the page, though fluorescent models are also available. Desk lights may be freestanding or clamped to the desk or shelf.
Good for: specific task lighting
Not for: general lighting
Dimmer switches modify the level of light and can alter the mood of a room. They can substitute for a conventional one- or two-way light switch, or be fitted to table or floor lamps.
Good for: lowering the light to create atmosphere or for soft light at night
Not: a substitute for a proper lighting plan
Downlighters are recessed ceiling lights with a strong downward beam. Flush fittings, where the bulb is level with the surround to give general light, are also built into the ceiling. As you'll need to allow from 6 to 8 inches (14 to 20 cm) for clearance, downlighters are best planned at the building stage, used in single or upper-storey rooms where they can be recessed into the roof space, or fitted into a false ceiling. It is possible to semi-recess and even surface-mount some downlighters, but this tends to concentrate the light.
Good for: creating pools of light to give atmosphere and, if used in sufficient numbers, for general light

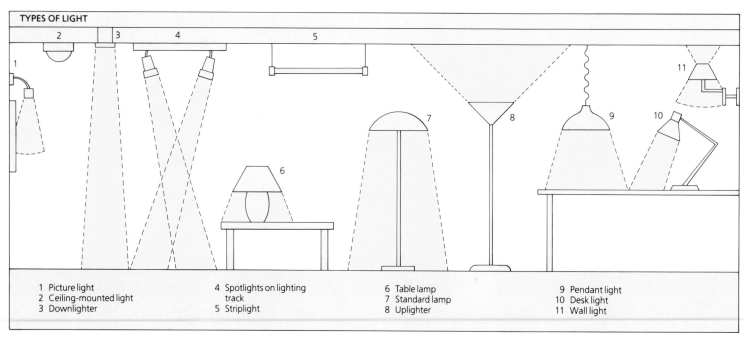

TYPES OF LIGHT		
1 Picture light	4 Spotlights on lighting track	6 Table lamp
2 Ceiling-mounted light	5 Striplight	7 Standard lamp
3 Downlighter		8 Uplighter

9 Pendant light	
10 Desk light	
11 Wall light	

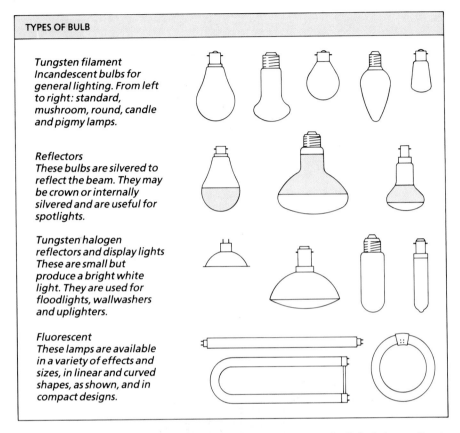

TYPES OF BULB

Tungsten filament
Incandescent bulbs for general lighting. From left to right: standard, mushroom, round, candle and pigmy lamps.

Reflectors
These bulbs are silvered to reflect the beam. They may be crown or internally silvered and are useful for spotlights.

Tungsten halogen
reflectors and display lights
These are small but produce a bright white light. They are used for floodlights, wallwashers and uplighters.

Fluorescent
These lamps are available in a variety of effects and sizes, in linear and curved shapes, as shown, and in compact designs.

Not for: task lighting, unless the light is immediately above a work surface

Lighting track, which forms a rail along which to move the light, helps spread illumination. The yard-(metre-) long tracks are fitted to a central lighting point and can be joined via a special connector to form straight runs or L-shape lengths. Lighting track is most commonly used with spotlights but it's possible to fit it with pendant lights too, using a pendant track adaptor.
Good for: making the most of a single lighting point
Not for: general lighting. Spotlights used to replace a central light can result in a combination of shadow and glare. Beam spotlights on to specific objects and areas and provide extra background light

Nightlights use a low (15) watt bulb to provide a dim but nevertheless constant source of light.
Good for: children's rooms
Not for: reading by

Pendant lights are connected by a length of flex (cord) to a ceiling rose (ceiling-mounted fitting) at the top and a lampholder at the other end. The lampholder carries both the bulb and the shade, which diffuses the light. Shades vary from paper lanterns and boxes to metal, fabric or glass domes

or globes. Two points to remember are that large shades decrease brightness, while lengthening the flex (cord) and fitting an opaque shade will concentrate the beam. (Rise and fall fittings are also available to adjust the height of pendant lights.) These lights need not be plain. In addition to the simple flex (cord) plus shade arrangement, there are chandeliers and elaborate multiple lights which need extra support to protect the flex (cord).
Good for: decoration and mood lighting
Not for: task or feature light

Picture lights are traditionally wall-mounted strip lights hidden by a curved metal baffle which directs light on to the painting. A spotlight positioned so that the beam illuminates the picture may substitute, but gives a harsher light.
Good for: mood and feature lighting
Not for: general light

Spotlights can be used on walls or ceilings, singly, in multiple fittings, or mounted on lighting track; desk and standard versions are also available. Spotlights can be angled to highlight specific features or light a particular area, or grouped in twos or threes to give more light.
Good for: feature, mood or task light
Not for: general light

Standard lamps are tall floor lamps with a shade or spotlights. Standard lamps with lights which swivel are useful because light can be redirected as required and raised to a suitable height for working or reading.
Good for: decoration, mood lighting or (adjustable lights only) task lighting
Not for: general light

Strip lights are linear lights popular for specific lighting in bathrooms and kitchens.
Good for: feature lighting hidden by a pelmet (valance) to emphasize curtains or inside a cupboard to display china; task lighting used on each side of a bathroom or dressing table mirror, in the bathroom in conjunction with a shaver socket and in the kitchen, concealed beneath top units
Not for: general lighting

Table lamps are predominantly decorative but they also help to create atmosphere. Most occasional tables are too low for table lamps; look for higher 'lamp' tables, especially if you intend to read or sew in the light. Conventional table lamps look best with shades no shorter than the base.
Good for: decoration and mood lighting; task lighting if carefully positioned
Not for: general lighting

Uplighters are wall or floor lamps with inverted shades; they throw light on to the ceiling which is then reflected to give indirect light. Uplighters which use tungsten halogen bulbs flood the ceiling with a bright white light.
Good for: creating atmosphere
Not for: task lighting or rooms where walls and ceilings are in poor repair

Wall lights may be spotlights, uplighters, bedside, strip or picture lights but in the main they are simply decorative. They should be fixed at between 66 and 72 inches (168 and 183 cm) from the floor to hide the bulb and prevent glare. Run wall lights from a separate lighting circuit so that they can be switched on in isolation from the central fitting.
Good for: almost every purpose, depending on the type of light fitting used and where it is placed

Wallwashers are directional downlighters. They are sometimes recessed eyeball spots and sometimes downlighters in partially reflective casing which directs the light. The indirect light is used to emphasize an area rather than a specific feature.
Good for: mood lighting and as a contribution to general lighting
Not for: task lighting

TYPES OF BULB

Choosing the correct bulbs (or lamps, as they are properly called in the UK) is essential if you're to get the most out of your lights. Some of the types listed here may not be available in the U.S.

Tungsten filament or incandescent lamps are available as candle, golf ball, mushroom, linear or globe shapes as well as the familiar pear-shaped bulb. They come in a choice of clear, pearl, opal or coloured finishes. Inside the glass casing is a filament, or coil, made from a metal called tungsten which can withstand repeated heating and cooling. (Tungsten filament bulbs are relatively inefficient because they produce a high ratio of heat to light.) The most popular wattages are 40, 60 and 100 watts but 15, 25, 75 and 150 are also available. It's important to use only the wattage specified by a light fitting (fixture) as too powerful a bulb may scorch the shade. Expect a light bulb to last for about 1000 hours though, because it is fragile, knocks may limit its life.

Reflectors, popular for spotlights, are tungsten filament bulbs which are silvered to direct the light. Crown-silvered (CS) bulbs from 40 to 100 watts are treated in front to direct the light back towards a reflector which projects it to create a narrow beam;

other types are silvered at the back to cast a wider beam. Parabolic (PAR) lamps are robust reflector bulbs with a wide, shallow crown for use with special fittings only because the heat produced is directed backwards.

Tungsten halogen lamps produce a powerful bright white light from a concentrated but powerful (250 to 500 watt) light source by using halogen, an inert gas. They are especially popular for uplighters where fittings conceal the glare. Tungsten halogen bulbs create considerable heat and should not be handled, so use them only where specified.

Fluorescent lamps come in more shapes and

Track-mounted spotlights and strip lighting fitted beneath the wall units (cabinets) create an efficient and attractive combination in this small, modern kitchen which is lacking in natural light.

Pendant lamps will direct the light down, if the shade is opaque, or up, if the top is transparent. They can be most effective hung low over a coffee table in place of table lamps.

for fluorescent bulbs, American bulbs are all a standard screw-in type.

WHAT SORT OF LIGHT DO I NEED?

Allow a minimum 20 watts per square yard or metre of floor if using tungsten bulbs, 10 watts if using fluorescent light, although this will vary depending on the purpose of the room you are lighting. This is sufficient for general lighting, but in addition you will need to provide feature lighting for emphasis, task lighting for work areas and mood lighting for atmosphere.

Routeways (passageways) need clear lighting for safety. Two-way switches upstairs and down, which work both hall and landing lights, together with a switch by the front door so that you turn on the hall light as soon as you come in, are essential to save negotiating stairs and passageways in the dark. Provide lighting in front of and above stairways, taking care to illuminate the edges of the stairs and any changes of level or flooring. Spotlights are useful for highlighting features or hazards but beware of creating areas of glare which alternate with pools of darkness. Wall lights, especially uplighters which direct light on to the ceiling so that it reflects on to the floor, are one option but remember that the light they give is indirect. Fit a dimmer switch to the landing light for a low level of illumination if you wish to leave it on all night or to prevent dazzle.

sizes than the familiar 4 ft (1200 mm) tube. There is now a variety of compact fluorescent lamps in the form of curved or double tubes and spherical or canister fittings, many of which are suitable replacements for tungsten filament bulbs, as well as the popular 1 and 1½ inch (25 and 38 mm) diameter linear fittings. Whatever their shape, they all produce light in quite a different way to incandescent bulbs. Fluorescent lamps generate ultra-violet radiation which reacts with chemicals painted on the inside of the tube to create light. They produce a higher amount of light for a lower wattage than tungsten filament bulbs so they are long-lasting (around 5000 hours) and cheap to run, though the initial cost is higher. They require special controls housed in the fitting or provided as a separate adaptor. Because the light they produce is 'cold', tinted versions, such as deluxe warm white, are a better choice for use in the home.

Fittings for conventional bulbs in the UK are either bayonet cap or Edison screw, both in two sizes. They are not interchangeable, so check new light fittings to see which type is required. Except

Work areas should have effective task lighting to supplement background light. The most important point to observe is that the lighting should illuminate the surface without creating glare. Make sure that the light will not shine in your eyes and that you cannot see the lamp. Kitchens need background lighting from downlighters, for example, plus extra light to illuminate the worksurface. This can be supplied from wall- or ceiling-mounted spots or strip lighting fitted beneath, and concealed by wall units (cabinets), or shielded by baffles. A study needs similar light directed on to the desk from a downlighter, or from a spotlight or desk light placed to reflect light on to the page without shining into your eyes.

Workshops, lofts (attics) and basements should have unequivocally bright light – a fluorescent tube with a diffuser to prevent glare will do – to avoid the hazards involved when using tools or, in the case of lofts (attics) and cellars, by a less familiar layout.

Living areas are the most difficult to light because they need to cater for the greatest variety of activities. You will need a combination of feature, task and mood lighting here, and you may have to add soft background lighting if the contrast between areas of light and dark is too pronounced. It's important to install a flexible lighting system so that you can vary the mood by turning different lights off, on or down. Start by concentrating on the sitting area where you will need 300-500 watts of light from downlighters, spotlights, wall lights, groups of pendant lights or a combination of types, depending on the size of the room.

Now consider task lighting. You will need a soft background light for watching television, light from a downlighter or reflected light from a spotlight for writing or playing the piano, and light from about 24

inches (60 cm) behind and slightly to one side from a spotlight, table, standard or pendant light for reading. Table lamps are frequently too small or placed too low to be effective, even for mood lighting. The bulb should be about 40 inches (100 cm) from the ground and must be shaded so that you cannot see it directly, whether you are standing or sitting. Mood lighting can also be created by fitting dimmer switches to table or central lights to throw certain areas into shadow or by using uplighters to cast light on to the ceiling. (Remember that this will also show up cracked plaster, wrinkled wallpaper – and cobwebs!) Wallwashers or directional downlights can be used either to illuminate a section of the room or for feature lighting, to highlight curtains or a wall of paintings, for example. For more specific feature lighting, choose carefully angled spotlights or pic-

Uplighters fitted with powerful tungsten halogen lamps cast a clear bright light and have a sculptural quality which suits many settings. Don't use them where plaster is in poor repair as they will highlight every crack!

A dressing room-style row of unshaded bulbs beside a mirror will direct light on to your face, where it's needed for making up. Strip lights placed each side of the glass work equally well.

ELECTRICAL TERMS

Alternating current or AC is the type of electricity supplied via the National Grid in the UK or the electrical utility companies in the US. (Direct current or DC is received via a generator or battery.)

Amps describes the rate of flow at which electricity is supplied.

Diffusers are baffles fitted to linear lights to disperse the light.

Earth leads are essential in metal lights, unless the metal parts are completely insulated from the user.

Ring circuits are created by a single cable from which all the outlets run. British homes have two circuits, one for lights and another for switch sockets. The average British domestic lighting circuit takes about 1000 watts – don't overload the circuit by installing too many fittings. An alternative is to use table, standard and track lighting connected to switch sockets to supplement a scheme. In the UK, wiring over 20 years old should be inspected. Homes in the US may have several different circuits controlling different switches, outlets and receptacles. Generally, these are rated at 15 or 20 amps – a figure that is marked on each fuse or circuit-breaker switch. Add the maximum wattage of each appliance on a given circuit, then divide by 120 to get the amperage and see if you can add more switches or receptacles to the circuit or if you must add a new circuit for new fixtures.

Units are measurements of electricity.

Voltage is the pressure at which electricity is supplied – 240 volts (UK), 110 (USA).

Watts mark the rate at which electricity is consumed. Each bulb should be marked with the number of watts it uses and light fittings (fixtures) should be compatible.

ture lights. You can also conceal strip lighting beneath a curtain pelmet (valance) or shelves or inside display cupboards.

Illuminate a dining table by a pendant light controlled by a dimmer switch hung low over the centre and install wall lights or downlighters to provide the general light needed when serving or showing guests to their seats. A rise-and-fall fitting (fixture) helps to direct the light, but make sure the shade will not get in the way. Similarly, measure the height of your room before you buy any fittings (fixtures) to ensure that there is sufficient head clearance.

Private places are where you can please yourself. High levels of light are only needed in task areas like the dressing table, bathroom mirror and when reading, writing or sewing. Light for making up or shaving by should be directed at your face, not at the mirror, so the best solution is to fit strip lights or dressing-room style rows of tungsten bulbs each side of the glass. These should be about 41 inches (105 cm) above the ground for use when sitting or 50 inches (150 cm) if you will be standing.

Bedside lights should be approximately 60 watts each, or up to 100 watts if masked by a dark shade. Wall-mounted lights should be about 30 inches (75 cm) and bedside lampshades 20 inches (50 cm) above the mattress to provide a comfortable reading light. Two-way switches which allow you to operate lights from the bedside or the door are useful and you may need to fit track lighting or spotlights to illuminate deep wardrobes.

Children's rooms need more flexible lighting, with a good level of general light from spotlights or wall lights for play, effective task lighting over desks, a nightlight or dimmer fitted to a main lighting source and bedside lights or spotlights for reading by. For safety, never fit a spotlight to a bunk or where a young child can touch the bulb.

Safety is even more important in bathrooms, where all light fittings should be water-resistant and operated by a switch outside or a pull-cord inside the door. Simple ceiling fittings (fixtures) are usually sufficient here, with the addition of strip lights or a spotlight to illuminate a mirror. You can obtain strip lights in the UK to fit over a bathroom mirror which incorporate a shaver socket – the only socket which should be fitted in the bathroom.

STYLE

There are two main styles of light fitting (fixture) – architectural, where the fitting (fixture) is hidden or

Left: Lights often need to be decorative as well as functional and should fit in with a room's decor. These lamps are correctly positioned on each side of the mirror, yet are also an attractive feature in keeping with the room's traditional style.

Below: An ingenious solution to the need for clear task lighting on a shared desk has been provided here. This clamp-mounted spotlight can swivel to direct light as required and its flexible stem bends to suit a variety of heights.

unobtrusive, and decorative, where the fitting forms a part of the room scheme. Most homes need a mixture of the two.

Architectural light fittings are suitable for every setting and are equally at home in an eighteenth-century house as in a modern apartment. Use architectural lights like downlighters, wallwashers, uplighters and spotlights to emphasize the features of a period home. Don't rely solely on period-style fittings like candelabra, chandeliers or converted gas lamps to provide enough light.

Decorative lights provide the centrepiece needed in period homes where the rooms have elaborate ceiling decorations or brackets for wall lights. Candle-style wall lights can take the place of candelabra (though you may do better to use real candles and light the area with concealed lights); etched glass bell shades on brass or wrought iron brackets are attractive in Victorian homes while Tiffany-style glass and beaded or fringed pendant shades look appropriately Art Nouveau in Edwardian ones.

Period fittings (fixtures) need not be frilly; look at Art Deco designs for a thirties-style house, or brass student's lamps (pendant and desk versions), plain brass spotlights and 'billiard' lights for an older one. Converted or reproduction oil or gas table and wall lamps are widely available, as are Victorian-style standard and coach lamps for exterior use but these should be used with discretion.

Many modern lights blur the distinction between architectural and decorative fittings (fixtures). Simple tungsten halogen table lamps and uplighters have a sculptural appeal, while high-tech interiors can display factory-type lead lamps, bulkhead lights or spotlights with baffles. One lighting classic, however, is the pottery table lamp, which is particularly effective when used in pairs (each side of a sofa, for example) to give symmetry to a scheme. They are available in a wide variety of styles from traditional ginger jar shapes with tasselled shades to fashionable spattered-pattern spheres for use with pleated or coolie shades.

Remember the standard lamp? Here is today's version, counterbalanced so that light can be directed where you want it and in a slim black shape that's right for the most avant-garde interior.

COLOUR

To see colour in a different light, view it under natural, tungsten filament, fluorescent and tungsten halogen light. The effect can be startling, but it's a useful exercise because before you buy fabric, paint or carpet, you should view the sample in daylight and in artificial light in the room where the material will be used.

Daylight changes with the aspect of the room. North-facing rooms are coldest, but give the clear light artists prefer. They need warmth, so choose colours like yellow, orange, pink, peach and cream. These colours are also effective in east-facing rooms which are sunny in the morning but tend to be cool. South- and west-facing rooms have a warm aspect and can take cooler colours like blue and green, though it's advisable to restrict these to accents in a cold climate and to choose a neutral like cream or buff for large areas like the walls. Pick a warmer colour for a west-facing room that's used in the morning, though you can afford a cooler colour for living rooms for afternoon and evening use. Choose as pale a carpet as is practical if the room is dark, because most of the light from the windows is directed on to the floor. If the carpet is dark it will absorb the light, but if it is light it will reflect it on to the walls and ceiling.

Tungsten filament light tends to emphasize warm colours like red and to drain the colour from greens and blues.

Fluorescent lamps should be chosen with care because they have the greatest effect on colour. The best choice for the home is a fluorescent like deluxe warm white (not the same thing as warm white) which emphasizes reds in a similar way to tungsten light. If you want to increase this effect, consider deluxe natural, while natural, widely used in offices, can be useful in rooms where daylight is limited. Avoid north light fluorescent lamps which give a cold blue light, and treat warm white, white or daylight tubes with caution. They emphasize yellow and green and can be unkind to faces as well as furnishings!

Tungsten halogen lamps project a bright white light which should be bounced off a surface to give indirect light as it's too powerful for direct use. The paler the surface the more intense the effect, so use with discretion in all white rooms.

Reflective values differ with each colour. Pale colours reflect light, dark ones absorb it, so figures vary from white, with a reflective value of 80 per cent, to olive green with under 10. The chart below shows how percentages can differ.

Colour	Reflective value
White	80
Off-white	70
Light apricot	66
Lemon	65
Cream	60
Light beige	56
Peach	53
Light apple	51
Mid-grey	43
Light blue	41
Deep pink	12
Olive green	9

Beaded Tiffany-style pendant lamps possess a charm that's all their own. These shades have fringes which catch the light; other versions are made from sections of coloured glass which refract it.

FACESAVERS
● Place a floor-mounted uplighter by a large plant to highlight its shape and illuminate a room's corner.
● Use two pendant lights over occasional tables in place of table lamps to save space.
● Fit a time switch to table lamps or use a light-sensitive lampholder so that lights are turned on automatically at dusk to deter burglars.
● Fit a double spotlight to a redundant (extraneous) centre light fitting (fixture) and angle the spots to highlight pictures or other features.
● Extend the flex (cord) of a pendant light and attach it to the ceiling with a hook or clip to centre it over a dining table. Use light spreader devices in the same way with several shades.
● Replace a cool fluorescent lamp with deluxe warm white for a more attractive effect.

CHAPTER 6

Window dressing

Choosing curtains is one of the most enjoyable aspects of furnishing a home. The window is the natural focal point of many rooms and the wealth of fabric, heading and track styles gives you scope to emphasize attractive features and camouflage faults. So what sort of treatment should you choose – or would the window look best uncovered? Here's how to decide.

WHAT STYLE IS YOUR HOME?

Period homes usually have smaller areas of window to cover because, before the widespread use of double glazing, warmth took priority over light. The typical English cottage may have very small windows indeed. Short, informal curtains are best for most true cottages and cottage-style homes, although those which have been extended and adapted may suit a more stately treatment.

Georgian and Victorian homes often have deep sash (double hung) windows which will be tall rather than wide, the easiest and most elegant shape to cover. The only problem is that there may be several identical windows in one wall. For the sake of symmetry, treat them separately. If the proportions are right you can afford to indulge in swags and tails or draped pelmets (valances) for a formal setting, curtain poles, pinch pleats and tie-backs for a pretty one. Beautiful windows shouldn't be overdressed, so be careful where you use frilly curtains and festoon blinds. Choose full-length curtains for elegance wherever possible. You may need to use short curtains where there is a deep sill, window seat or radiator but don't forget that blinds will also complement the shape of sash windows.

Modern homes tend to have windows which are wide rather than long. Formal, traditional window treatments can be difficult to adapt; swags and tails may look strange and tie-backs only work if you drape voluminous amounts of fabric over the windowpane. Curtain poles may sag if there are insufficient supports, so choose a pelmet (valance), pencil or pinch pleat heading if you want to use traditional curtains at wide windows. Simple curtains, full-length if possible and made from a generous amount of fabric, cannot fail to make an impact over such an area. If you prefer blinds, think about using two or three festoon or Roman blinds to cover one window because a single blind may look cumbersome and be difficult to raise. Alternatively, opt for a wide roller, Venetian or vertical louvre blind.

TYPES OF WINDOW

Casement windows open outwards. Sometimes both windows open, but frequently there is one opening and one fixed pane, plus a top light.

Fixed windows may be decorative or, like clerestory windows which are set in the wall near the ceiling line, admit light without affecting privacy.

Louvre or jalousie windows consist of horizontal glass panes which open outwards. Louvre windows rarely need covering, but as it's easy to dislodge the entire set from the outside they should only be used for very small windows to minimize the security risk.

Ranch windows are like clerestory windows set lower down but still higher than conventional windows. They may be fixed or opening.

Sash or double-hung windows slide up and down. When these windows are found in period homes, they should be restored or replaced by copies, not by casement windows, when necessary. Georgian windows tend to have more and smaller panes than later types, and in some sash windows the cross bars have been removed. Try to find out what the original windows were like.

Sliding windows are popular in America and are widely used in both the UK and USA as patio doors. They are ideal to frame a good view.

Skylights are set into the roof and may be of the opening or fixed type.

PROBLEM WINDOWS

Although most windows fall into one of the above categories, styles may vary widely – and can sometimes be difficult to dress.

Arched windows need thought. Modern versions can be covered by curtains on curved track, fixed vertically to follow the arch, but classic arched and Gothic style windows look best if curtains are mounted unobtrusively above the window, drawing right back from it. Shutters are another solution if they were the original fitting, or dispense with a covering and let the window speak for itself.

Bay windows need curtains which follow the shape of the bay or separate blinds over each section, useful when there's a radiator or window seat

Imaginative window treatments not only emphasize your style but cope with practical problems like screening the room from sun – or passers-by. Here plain cream blinds with a fan shape finish create a dashing but economical window covering.

Treat a shallow bay by filling the area with a window seat and hanging sill-length curtains at every pane. The frilled pelmet (valance) gives importance to the scheme and is trimmed to match the cord tie-backs for an elegant, traditional look.

beneath. Combine the two, using blinds to filter light during the day and full-length curtains simply for show or to cover the area at night. You *can* cut off the bay by hanging curtains straight across it but this may leave the bay looking bare during the day and it wastes space when the curtains are closed.

Bow windows need a treatment which complements the curve. Full-length curtains with a ruffled pelmet and tie-backs look attractive.

Corner windows are sometimes found in houses built between the wars. If curtains are required, fit them on separate lengths of track which draw clear of each window. (Curved track can be used, but it won't fit snugly.) Decorative angled windows in

halls or living rooms are best left uncovered.

Dormer windows, which project from the roof, are usually small. Make the most of the light by choosing track which curves back on to the side of the dormer so that the (short) curtains can draw clear of the window, or make sure that they are not too full. Alternatively fit a blind.

French doors need curtains or a blind which draws well clear of the opening. Consider full-length curtains secured by tie-backs for a traditional scheme, a Roman or vertical louvre blind for a modern one.

Picture windows have large panes designed to make the view a focal point of the room, so there's little point in covering them with nets or sheer curtains unless you need to preserve your privacy. If the window space takes up two-thirds of the wall or more, curtain the entire wall for impact.

Pivoting windows are difficult because they may obstruct the curtains. Choose curtains or vertical louvre blinds which draw clear of the pane or fit a top-mounted blind if there is sufficient clearance.

Skylights seldom need curtains for privacy, but you may want to mask the black space at night. In this case fit simple roller blinds and secure the lower edge with hooks when drawn.

... AND WINDOW PROBLEMS

Some difficult situations have nothing to do with the shape of the window. Here are some examples.

Problem: The window affords a view inside the house and needs screening during the day.

Solution: Fit an inner curtain or blind which filters the light. Consider lace panels for a traditional room, sheer blinds, a vertical louvre or a Venetian blind. Café curtains which cover the lower half of the window look attractive in kitchens, while jardinières which curve upwards to clear the base of the window are a pretty solution in traditional living and dining rooms. Inner curtains of lace or net look best hung from lightweight track which can be attached to the outer track.

Problem: There is a single small window in your room which has been set into a long wall.

Solution: Choose from several options. First, why not leave the window uncovered? Paint the frame a colour which co-ordinates with the walls, choosing a darker or lighter version of the paint colour or picking out an accent of the wallcovering for emphasis. The second solution is to fit shutters, painted to match the wall and frame. Thirdly, make the window merge with the wall by fitting an unobtrusive roller blind to match the paint or wallcovering. Finally, consider using full-length curtains.

Problem: The window is a door.

Solution: Fit a full-length portière curtain which draws to one side and secure it with a tie-back.

Problem: There are two windows in the same wall.

Solution: It's often a good idea to treat them as one unit, unless they are wildly disproportionate, some distance apart, or period sash windows. Fit a continuous length of track, if possible, and if they differ in height choose full-length curtains (or drapes) to mask the problem.

Problem: There is a radiator beneath the window.

Solution: This is only a problem if you want to have curtains (or drapes) rather than blinds. Either fit short curtains which skim the top of the radiator or vent or, if full-length ones are more in keeping with your scheme, opt for show curtains permanently fixed in place by tie-backs and use a festoon or Roman blind to cover the pane. You can buy curtain poles designed to stand clear of projecting sills or extension brackets for use with curtain track which make it easier to fit full-length curtains.

Problem: The windows in the room differ in size.

Solution: Treat all the windows in the same way as

Let distinctive windows like these speak for themselves. Here curved windows have been given very discreet, dark curtains on rods – almost invisible – and each recess has been painted black to emphasize the window's graceful shape.

the largest, unless the odd one out is a decorative, or very tiny window, as chopping and changing lengths distracts the eye. You need not use full-length drapes at every window to balance those at French or patio doors but make sure that all the other windows have curtains the same length. Leave ornamental windows uncovered and fit co-ordinating roller blinds to cover very small windows or roof lights.

Problem: The window has a dismal view.
Solution: Fix glass or wooden shelves over a small window and add plants which will flourish in the light or glass ornaments which will reflect it. Cover larger windows with figured sheer or lace curtains or blinds which will admit light when drawn. Alternatively, use Venetian or vertical louvre blinds. Go outside too. Paint a trompe l'oeil design on a facing wall or train attractive climbing plants across the window if it's not essential for light – or fit a window box. Crammed with flowers, it will look splendid, will screen the ugly view and will scent the air at the same time.

Problem: The window lets in draughts.
Solution: The remedy here is to treat the window rather than the drapes – but you can help to conserve heat by choosing insulated lining or thermal blinds designed to direct heat back into the room, or by using heavy curtains with lining and interlining to repel draughts.

Problem: The window faces east and I don't want to wake up at dawn.
Solution: Medium or heavyweight lined curtains are essential for unwilling early risers unless you are prepared to use a light-resistant roller blind with

Drape a dormer with a swathe of sheer fabric suspended from a narrow pole and tie it to one side for a simple but attractive solution to this problem window. Allow the fabric to fall to the floor for maximum effect.

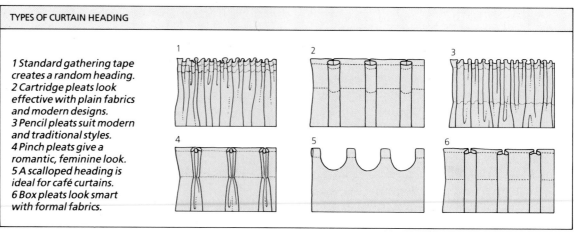

TYPES OF CURTAIN HEADING

1 Standard gathering tape creates a random heading.
2 Cartridge pleats look effective with plain fabrics and modern designs.
3 Pencil pleats suit modern and traditional styles.
4 Pinch pleats give a romantic, feminine look.
5 A scalloped heading is ideal for café curtains.
6 Box pleats look smart with formal fabrics.

light drapes. Choose 'thick white' (also known as blackout) lining to keep out the light or go for a coloured lining to contrast with plain curtains or to pick up a colour in the design of patterned ones; trim the curtains to match for co-ordination.

Problem: I like to open the window for ventilation but the curtains flap in the breeze.
Solution: Choose medium-weight curtains which draw clear of the window and fit weights to the hem to ensure that they hang well. Tie-backs will keep them in place but should only be added if appropriate to the style of the room.

WINDOW TREATMENTS

There's more to dressing a window than choosing the fabric and running up curtains! What about headings, valances, trims, tracks and blinds? An increasing number of treatments previously confined to professionals are now available for home sewing. Here are some of the most popular.

CURTAINS

From full-length, lined curtains to swathes of sheer fabric or café curtains, the choice is endless.
The heading sets the style and dictates the amount of material required. Some elaborate headings are sewn by hand but most curtains today use ready-made gathering tape with cords which pull the curtain up into the appropriate style.
Standard gathering tape is ideal for short, lightweight curtains; allow at least 1½ times the width of the track (not the window) when estimating the amount of fabric you'll need.
Cartridge pleats give a full round pleat (especially if you pack the pleat with tissue paper for a few days when the curtains are first pulled up) and look particularly smart in modern settings. You'll find that they require twice the track width in fabric.
Pencil pleats give a slim pleat with a tall upright heading, needing 2¼ to 2½ times the track width.
Pinch pleats (available in a choice of depths) and elaborate smocked effects need 2 to 3 times the track width, depending on the manufacturer's recommendations. Pinch pleat tape, which uses special long triple hooks, needs 1¾ times the track width. You can afford to economize a little when using a heavy fabric because otherwise the curtains may cover too much of the pane when drawn back. Never be stingy with cheap or lightweight fabrics; you'll require 3 times the width of the track with

nets or sheers, for example. If in doubt, always overestimate.
Scalloped headings, traditionally used with café curtains, are cheapest of all, but require skill and effort in place of tape, hooks or multiple widths, so be sure of your talents before you start.

Length should be to the floor, to the radiator, or to the sill. Traditionally, full-length curtains should be

A Roman blind is a practical and stylish way to cover French windows. Soften the effect with full-length curtains secured by tie-backs and trimmed to match; economize, if necessary, by making them purely for show.

1 inch (2.5 cm) above the floor, and though the recent fashion for trailing draperies has changed that, you may be wise to save treatments which end in pools of fabric for fixed drapes or you will constantly need to rearrange, and clean, the curtains.

The quantity of fabric is decided by the type of heading, as well as by the overall size of the curtains, so you must always choose the heading before you buy the fabric. You should also take the pattern repeat into account, where applicable, as all widths should match. Allow one complete repeat for every width except the first. For example, if you need four widths, allow three repeats. You will need to add on up to an extra 12 inches (30 cm) to the overall width of the curtains for turns and side seams, if joining widths. If you use standard heading tape on short curtains, add an extra 8 inches (20 cm) for hems and headings, and allow up to 15 inches (37.5 cm) for deep headings on full-length curtains. In addition, each length of pile fabric (such as velvet) should hang the same way. It's always worth buying an extra half yard or metre of fabric for trims and tie-backs.

To estimate the amount of fabric, follow the instructions below.

1 Measure the width of the track.

2 Multiply by the number of widths the curtain heading dictates (plus seam allowance).

3 Divide by the width that the fabric is sold in – you will have to check that first. Round up to the nearest full measurement. The total figure is the number of widths you will require.

4 Measure the length of the curtains, including an allowance for hems and headings.

5 Multiply by the number of widths required (the total you arrived at in Step 3).

6 Add on an allowance for the pattern repeat and round your total figure up to the nearest half yard or metre.

EXAMPLE

1 Width of track	8 ft (2.4 m)

2 Say you have chosen cartridge pleats which require twice the track width. Multiply the above figure by 2   16 ft (4.8 m)

3 Divide by fabric width (e.g. 48 in/120 cm) and round up   4 widths

4 Length of curtains, plus hem and heading allowance   6 ft 8 in (2m)

5 Multiply by number of widths (i.e. 4)

26 ft 8 in (8 m)

6 Add on allowance for pattern repeat (e.g. 6 in/15 cm repeat – for 4 widths, allow 3 repeats, i.e. 18 in/45 cm)   28 ft 2 in (8.45 m)

Round up to nearest foot or half metre to find total fabric required   28 ft 6 in (8.5 m)

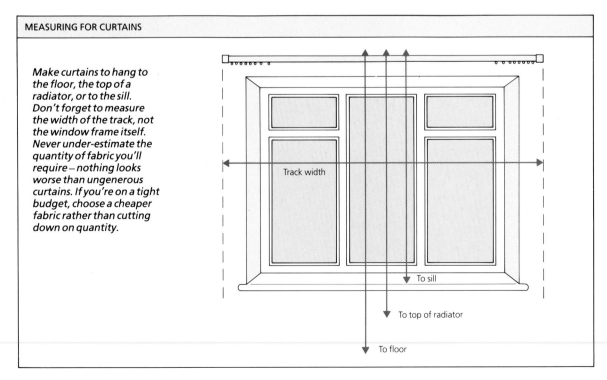

MEASURING FOR CURTAINS

Make curtains to hang to the floor, the top of a radiator, or to the sill. Don't forget to measure the width of the track, not the window frame itself. Never under-estimate the quantity of fabric you'll require – nothing looks worse than ungenerous curtains. If you're on a tight budget, choose a cheaper fabric rather than cutting down on quantity.

Track width

To sill

To top of radiator

To floor

Unusual windows demand inventive treatments. These Roman blinds which draw up into soft pleats are the perfect solution to this window problem and can be made fron any lightweight curtain fabric.

A delightful solution to a difficult window: these drapes are secured at the apex of the triangle and at each side and finished with a tasselled fringe. A border defining the recess emphasizes the window's shape.

All-in-one linings are easier to make. They are cut about 1 inch (2.5 cm) shorter than the curtain fabric all round and sewn back to back with it. When the side seams and hem are in place the 'bag' is turned right side out.

Detachable linings are useful if you intend to wash the curtains because they eliminate the danger of different rates of shrinkage – but don't expect them to hang as well as the sewn-in sort.

Tracks, poles and pelmets (or valances) should complement the curtains. This hardware is important because the length of the track is one of the items which determines the amount of fabric that's required. Make sure that the track extends at least 6 inches (15 cm) on each side of the window. (The fuller the curtains, the more track you will need.) Remember to allow more for round curtain poles or rods because curtains only draw as far as the end bracket, not the finial (decorative endpiece) on the end. You'll also need to choose fittings to suit the weight of your curtains – don't expect light plastic curtain track to bear the weight of full-length lined drapes, for instance.

Tracks are made from metal or plastic and can usually be cut or ordered at the required length. The most popular colour is white, though gold and decorated trim is available, especially in versions with a rounded moulding which imitate poles. Some track can be painted, and there are several grades to cater for heavy, medium or lightweight curtains. You'll need to know if the track can be used with deep headings if required and if it can be used in the appropriate place, whether that's the ceiling, wall or inside the window recess. Many tracks can be bent to cope with a bay window, but the maximum angle differs with the brand. Cording sets are available for curved track as well as straight runs, or you could use draw rods which hang behind the curtains for heavy fabrics. Light nylon track is designed for net or sheer curtains and can be fixed by extension brackets to the underside of the window or to the wall in conjunction with curtain track. Accessories like cording sets (to store excess cord), overlaps (to ensure the curtains close completely) and finials are widely available.

Poles are designed to be seen. They are made from metal (usually brass effect), plastic (metallic, white or wood finish) or stained, lacquered or untreated wood; some plastic and wooden poles can be painted to suit your decor. A wide window needs two or more lengths of pole joined by a support

Lining makes curtains hang better, prevents seams from showing through light materials and protects the fabric from the effects of condensation and sunlight. You needn't bother to line kitchen and bathroom curtains which need frequent laundering (permanently lined curtains should be dry-cleaned because the lining and outer fabric may shrink at different rates if washed), and you shouldn't line sheers, which are designed to filter the light. Every other style benefits from being lined.

Locked-in linings are slip-stitched to the curtain fabric at about 4 inch (10 cm) intervals to give a professional touch.

bracket and, as with track, it's important to buy a heavy-duty type for use with full-length lined curtains. Poles usually look best affixed to the wall, but if this cannot be done it's often possible to secure them to the ceiling. Wooden poles can be cut and some poles can be corded, while versions are now available to fit a bay window.

Tension rods made from wood or plastic compress to fit inside an alcove or window frame. They are used with curtain rings or café curtains.

Pelmets (or valances) cover curtain track, add importance to curtains and help to balance a high ceiling. They can be made from fabric, fabric-covered board, or painted wood. Frilled fabric pelmets (these soft types are also called valances in the US) can be made with gathering tape and fixed with a valance rail which clips to the front of curtain track. Various styles of pelmet (valance) – serpentine, arched, and scalloped – are cut from fabric-covered board, while informal pelmets (valances) are simply painted to blend or contrast with the colour scheme. Variations on the theme include swags and tails made from fabric draped over a board or pole, stapled in place, and finished with long side pieces (the tails, or jabots). Although modern versions are less stiff than the traditional swags and tails this is still a very grand window treatment. More formal still is the lambrequin, where the wooden or fabric-covered pelmet (valance) is extended to form a three-sided box.

Draping fabric

This is a stylish window treatment which is also economical because only single widths of fabric are used. The technique is similar to that for making swags and tails; simply wind the fabric round a curtain pole and allow it to trail over the floor. Use one length of curtain secured in the centre or two meeting in symmetrical falls for an impromptu swag and tails effect but keep to lightweight fabrics like nets, sheers and light cottons which will drape well and stay in place. Heavy materials are too bulky and silky ones are difficult to manipulate. Above all, remember that a window treatment is not a window covering. Reserve drapes for windows which are not overlooked or combine them with co-ordinating blinds to preserve your privacy.

Blinds

Blinds show off the shape of windows and are a practical choice where space is limited.

Austrian blinds are one of the prettiest kinds.

PELMETS AND VALANCES

The pelmets on the left are made from plain or fabric-covered board; those on the right are gathered material hung from a valance rail attached to curtain track. Choose a pelmet that's in keeping with the style of the room and of the curtains, teaming cotton prints with a valanced pelmet or painted board, sheers with a filmy scalloped design and velvet with covered board, for example. Don't forget the importance of trimmings to add co-ordination and a professional finish.

Lace panels or blinds protect your privacy and are perfect for feminine or traditional rooms. Remember that you may need another window covering at night. Consider full-length curtains, or shutters, as shown here.

Venetian blinds make a chic window covering for minimal modern schemes – look for the fine or 'micro' (miniblind) version. They're versatile too, as the slats can be angled to filter the light, as here, or closed to exclude it.

Less elaborate than festoons, they pull straight when closed except for the decorative ruffle at the base. Because they are gathered from side to side they require extra width as well as fabric for the frill; allow at least 2¼ times the width of the window. Light fabrics are best for these ruffled blinds and they look particularly attractive with contrasting piping which picks up a colour in the design or relates to the overall scheme.

Festoon blinds are lovely and traditional, but because they are gathered vertically as well as from side to side they may need more fabric than curtains. Light and sheer fabrics are recommended for

both Austrian and festoon blinds, not only because of the weight but because these ruffled blinds will obscure much of the window even when raised.

Roller blinds are the most popular. They can be bought ready made, cut to size, or made to order. There's a wide range of plain colours, patterns and border designs, many of which form part of co-ordinated furnishing ranges. It's also possible to make your own roller blinds with strong cotton and spray-on fabric stiffener, but it can be difficult to achieve an even crispness.

Roman blinds pull up into pleats. Professionally made Roman blinds often have wooden dowels or

This small window gains importance from its treatment. A simple print roller blind fits just inside the recess, while the trellis acts as a frame and the arrangement on the sill becomes an integral part of the 'picture'.

colours are popular today, especially in the US where they have taken over from the wider type; mirrored and multicoloured effects are also available. Use Venetian blinds in modern sitting and dining rooms as well as kitchens and home offices for a sleek, high-tech look.

Vertical louvre blinds have vertical slats made from plastic or stiffened fabric. They can be closed completely, drawn as curtains, or angled to filter the light.

Wooden and bamboo blinds make attractive screens and room dividers as well as window coverings. Some types do not pull up and are meant purely for show and others (particularly those with wooden slats) occupy considerable space at the top of the window. Check before you buy. Bamboo blinds do not afford much privacy at night, especially if a light is switched on behind them.

COLOUR AND PATTERN

Curtains and blinds can do more than just cover the window. They should contrast or co-ordinate with the room scheme – and add impact. If you have a patterned carpet, repeat one of the dominant colours in plain curtain fabric or choose fabric with a discreet geometric motif, like a trellis design, or a self pattern. If the carpet is plain or yet to be chosen, you can afford to choose a stronger pattern. Take into account the effect of advancing and receding colours and remember that bold designs usually look best used over a large area while small patterns suit small windows. If the room is small too, or particularly busy, match the windows to the walls by choosing the same plain colour or a closely coordinating pattern for both. Fabric and wallpaper designs are rarely exactly the same because the materials differ in width. British wallpaper is generally 21 inches (53 cm) wide, curtain fabric 47 inches (120 cm). American wallpaper can vary from 18 inches (46 cm) to 54 inches (142 cm) wide; fabrics vary from 36 inches (91 cm) to 54 inches (142 cm) wide. Don't forget the trim. Incorporate colours used in the fabric design or elsewhere in the room to pipe tie-backs and pelmets (valances) and trim curtains. Pick up one of the colours in patterned fabric for lining, scatter cushions or a coordinating blind. Look for fabrics which co-ordinate with wallcoverings, borders, bedlinen and nets or sheer curtains for a foolproof scheme or opt for the precision of shutters or miniblinds in bright colours to add a splash of contrast or neutrals for a cool modern look.

bars to define the pleats but home-made blinds usually omit these for a softer effect. Choose Roman blinds if you want a less stark look than that given by roller blinds without the fussiness of festoons. They are also perfect for making the most of expensive material as they give maximum impact for the minimum of fabric.

Venetian blinds have horizontal metallic slats which can be adjusted to screen as well as to exclude the light. Slimline slats (miniblinds) in bright

FACESAVERS

- Always sew curtain hems before the heading to ensure that they hang well.
- Use 'invisible' thread so that stitches don't show.
- Use Velcro to attach the edges of detachable lining to the outer curtain.
- Drape curtains when first hung so that they fall correctly. Tug gently at the hem and arrange the curtain so that it falls in natural pleats. Tie loosely to hold in position for 24 hours.
- Curtains too short? Add a frill or a border to make up the length, or consider converting full-length curtains to sill length and turning short drapes into café curtains, perhaps with scalloped headings.
- You've let the hem down and it's all too obvious? There's bound to be a discrepancy in the colour of fabric that's shaded from sunlight and the area that's open to view. Capitalize on it by sewing patterned braid which contains both shades along the line. Add accessories in both colours and use the braid on cushions or for tie-backs too.
- Not enough fabric? Curtains aren't compulsory! There is sure to be a style of blind to suit your room scheme. As a substitute you could make a Roman blind which folds into soft pleats and is economical on fabric.
- Uninspiring curtains? Pep them up with contrasting trim. Sew a ruffle and matching tie-backs or add straight braid (remember to mitre the corners). For instant results, rehang the curtains and draw both to one side with a tasselled tie-back. Loop another tassell to the same side of the pole or track to emphasize the effect.
- Ugly curtain track? Make a pelmet (valance) to cover it from matching material, co-ordinating fabric-covered board or painted wood.

Austrian blinds and curtains which sweep the floor add up to a lovely traditional treatment. Choose co-ordinating fabrics for surefire results; the trellis print on blinds and seat cushions is specifically designed to complement the curtains.

CHAPTER 7

Borderlines

How can you co-ordinate wall and window patterns without using wallpaper? What should you do to reconcile different colours? How can you increase the impact of bedlinen or blinds?

Answer: add a border or frieze. You can buy ready-made paper borders and fabric trim for curtains and cushions, or you can stencil your own. You can use them to give definition at ceiling or skirting (baseboard) height, to imitate a dado, picture rail or panels, to substitute for missing mouldings or to correct the proportions of a room.

WALLS

A frieze is usually wider and more pictorial than a border but there's no absolute distinction between the two. The widths of borders and friezes vary from around ¾ inch to 17½ inches (18 to 450 mm) and the pattern may be printed on wallpaper, vinyl (plain or ready-pasted), polyethylene film (Nova-mura), or made from paper and plastic (Lincrusta).

The proportions of a room can be altered or emphasized by the way the border is used.

If the ceiling is too high create a false picture rail using a medium-width or deep border or frieze, or use a border at cornice and skirting (baseboard) level and paint the wall a darker colour to reduce its apparent height.

If the room has an interesting cornice use a narrow border in a discreet design immediately beneath it for emphasis.

If the room originally had an interesting cornice, add a border with an architectural design (Greek key or acanthus, for example) to replace it. Emphasize the effect if the ceiling is high by adding a co-ordinating frieze to substitute as a picture rail.

If there are long stretches of wall, in a hall or long living room, for example, create a dado by either using a frieze at chair rail level or adding a border or wooden moulding to separate two co-ordinating wallcoverings, or paper above with paint below. Position the border about one-third of the way up the wall for the correct proportions.

If the room is large and featureless consider an old traditional device – paper panels to add interest and act as a substitute for pictures and possessions, which take time to collect.

If you want to emphasize or enlarge a window or mirror you could try surrounding it with a frieze to form an additional frame.

The pattern should relate to the style of the room. A cool-coloured acanthus design may be appropriate in a Georgian or neo-classical setting, for example, while a jazzy frieze goes well in a Memphis-inspired room. Fruit and flowers suit all settings, but you could go for specialized designs, such as sea-shells for a bathroom or an alphabet for a nursery. Take care when choosing friezes for children's rooms. It's easy to be swayed by delightful nursery designs or a toddler's passion for the Muppets but remember that these patterns have a short life. Paste the border on to eggshell (alkyd semigloss) paint rather than wallpaper and you have some chance of removing it without dis-

It's not essential to change the wallcovering when creating a dado, and retaining the same pattern can increase the sense of space. Here the division is marked just as effectively by a pastel-painted moulding topped by a co-ordinating frieze.

turbing the rest of the decor. The alternative is to choose a design which will be equally acceptable to an older child.

Remember that using a patterned border with companion curtain or cushion fabric is one of the easiest ways to achieve a co-ordinated room. Use in conjunction with patterned wallpaper for a dressy look, or with self-patterned or painted walls for a simpler effect. A contrasting colour in panels or stripes on plain walls will create pattern, or find a border with a motif which relates to a theme elsewhere in the room (on china or curtains, for instance) like roses or bows. Don't be afraid to use two borders together for effect to replace architectural details like a cornice with a companion picture rail. You can also employ two to give definition, by using a narrow border above and beneath a wide one, or to emphasize a particular colour.

PAINT OR PAPER?

Stencils have the advantage that you can create designs to your own specification. Ready-cut stencils are now widely available but you don't have to rely on manufactured designs. You have more flexibility about where to use stencilled borders (they can be curved as well as straight, for example, or used over relief wallcoverings like Anaglypta or woodchip) and, of course, you can choose the colours. On the other hand, more work is involved in stencilling and it's difficult to achieve elaborate effects. You cannot hope to remove a stencilled border without papering or painting over it, and if you use signwriting paint for definition it may be difficult to obliterate.

Printed borders and friezes contain more colours than the average stencilled design. They are easy to put up and not too difficult to remove. The chief problem is that they are only available in a limited range of designs and colourways and there may not be a border to match the furnishings you choose. Seams may be noticeable and because paper borders are not as durable as painted ones, they may be susceptible to peeling or tearing.

For a stencilled border you will need soft chalk, a stencil design cut from acetate or thick cardboard, masking tape or photomount spray, paint (emulsion – called latex in America – or signwriter's paint for walls, gloss for furniture), a special stumpy stencil brush (available from art shops) and a saucer.
Method First, work out where the stencil is going. (Use soft chalk to mark a top or base line in case you

Left: Stencilled friezes are hard-wearing and versatile. This simple bathroom gains distinction from a frieze painted above the tiles and along the bath panel – an easy way to brighten up an existing colour scheme.

Below: This clever furniture arrangement and colour scheme turn a simple sofa and shelf unit into something special. The pattern of the sofa cushions is repeated by the frieze which runs along the wall at picture-rail level and beneath each shelf.

Deco-style stencilled fans create a thirties setting, emphasized by the oval lamp, cocktail shaker and vase. The colours – green, yellow and apricot – are carefully chosen to evoke the period.

waver.) Now fix the stencil in place with masking tape. (Stick the tape to clothing once or twice to remove excess stickiness so the surface of the wall won't be damaged when you remove it. If you are stencilling on to paper use photomount spray to fix the stencil lightly in place.) Decant a little paint into the saucer and work it well into the bristles of the stencil brush. Dab the brush on to a scrap of paper a few times to remove surplus paint and then fill in the stencil by dabbing rather than brushing to and fro. Don't use too much paint or it may bleed from one cut-out to the next. If you are using more than one colour you'll need a saucer and stencil brush for each, and if the stencil is elaborate you will have to apply one colour at a time to avoid runs. Allow each to dry before applying the next.

Cutting a stencil It's not difficult to adapt a design from a print on fabric or wallpaper, provided you remember that each part and colour must be separated by a white area where the 'ties' between cut-outs occur. In other words, the stencil will not be an exact representation of the print, no matter how good your artistic skills. It's not possible to omit the ties, because without them the colours will run together into a blob, as any child who's done potato printing will tell you.

For your first attempt, choose a simple design with broad ties which won't break and leave a wide border above and below to give the stencil strength. The design you choose doesn't have to be the same size as the finished stencil because it's easily enlarged on a photocopier. Transfer the design on to stencil card (from art shops) using carbon paper. You can trace it on to acetate, which is transparent and easy to clean, but it is more flimsy and may be more difficult to control than cardboard. Next place the card or acetate on a board and cut out the design with a special craft knife, taking care to preserve the ties. Remember to keep the original design in case you damage the stencil – some can be exceedingly fragile.

Your wallpaper border may be ready-pasted vinyl or polyethylene film, but although the pasting techniques may differ (follow the manufacturer's instructions for acceptable results), those for cutting and affixing are the same.

Method The first step is to mark the position of the border in soft chalk. Use a spirit level to help get it straight but let your eye be the final judge. If the picture rail is out of true, affix the frieze so that it looks right in relation to it rather than risk a divergence between the two. Now cut the frieze as required and concertina it, folding pasted edge to pasted edge, to make it easy to carry. Where necessary, butt join the ends so that the pattern matches, and finish by pressing into place with a seam roller.

MAKING PANELS

Fake panels are a cheap and easy way of dressing walls. Mark the position of each panel with soft chalk because their shape can have a dramatic effect on the proportions of the room. Tall, narrow panels will make it look higher, while wide shapes will emphasize the horizontal. On a bare wall you can mix the two if your scheme allows, combining a dado or wide base panel with two or three tall ones above. Aim for symmetry, keeping panels which are the same shape the same size, or flanking a large central panel with two identical ones on each side.
Method Mark the four sides of the panel, using a plumb bob and line to determine vertical lines and a spirit level to check horizontals. Then step back to assess the effect and alter the lines if necessary. If the panels are narrow cover the centre with wallpaper if wanted, but restrict this treatment to panels less than one width of wallpaper, which is 18 to 21 inches (46 to 53 cm) across, as seams will spoil the effect. Now fix the first length of border to the left hand vertical (vice versa if you are left-handed), allowing an extra 1 inch (2.5 cm) at each end. Next paste the first horizontal in place, allowing the same overlap. Mitre the corner by placing a ruler over the diagonal where the two lengths meet and cutting across with a trimming knife. You'll be left with a corner of paper on top which can be removed and a second piece beneath the horizontal strip which should be peeled back for access. Smooth the corners back into place and complete the panel.

FLOORS

Stencilling is a traditional method of decorating floorboards. You can create a border to repeat the pattern of a wall frieze or a motif used elsewhere in the room, or create a trompe l'oeil rug in the centre (particularly effective in a living or dining room). It's not essential to use gloss paint, but you must protect the finish with at least three coats of clear polyurethane varnish to preserve your handiwork.

FURNITURE

Brighten up old and new furniture with a base coat of gloss or eggshell paint or varnish and finish it with

Top: By creating your own stencils you can transfer a motif from fabric or wallpaper for instant co-ordination. Stencils add pattern to floorboards – protect with floor-quality varnish.

Above: Wallpaper borders combine more colours than it's practical to do when stencilling; prints from co-ordinated ranges are ideal if you want an exact match with textiles or wallcovering.

Sit up in bed and look out over the Mediterranean, not just for a two-week holiday but every morning of the year. The humour of this trompe l'oeil masterpiece is reinforced by the blue walls and ceiling and the seagull hovering in mid-air.

a stencil. Stencil floral wreaths around the handles of a nondescript chest of drawers, or decorate cupboard doors with two centrally placed motifs. Finish a toy chest with a nursery design and turn a fibreboard storage unit into a work of art by adding a distinctive border.

FABRIC

Borders give soft furnishings a professional finishing touch. Use plain piping in a contrasting colour or one which relates to the design to define pelmets (valances), tie-backs, table linen, cushions and loose covers; frills and fabric borders to add interest to curtains; tassels to secure drapes and finish covers; traditional gimp or braid to complete lampshades. Trimmings such as these are important because they finish your furnishings and give you the opportunity to emphasize existing colour or introduce new ones to co-ordinate or contrast with the scheme.

Luckily, it's never too late to add the final touch. A pair of tasselled, piped or braided tie-backs can make a vast difference to a droopy pair of curtains: you can use co-ordinating plain fabric on patterned curtains, a contrasting pattern on plain if there's no material to match. Stitch piping or braid which brings in the colours of curtains, carpet or walls to cushions or blinds which don't do much for your scheme; make piped, frilled, box pleated or plain valances, tablecloths, cushions or loose covers, and watch your colour scheme come to life. Remember that you can stencil on fabric using fabric paint in pastels, bright colours or fluorescent effects to create your own design. Simply stencil your pattern, iron the design to set it and wash with care.

TROMPE L'OEIL AND MURALS

If the idea of a border appeals to you, but you're looking for something more dramatic, why not investigate trompe l'oeil and murals?

Trompe l'oeil means 'deceives the eye'. Skilled painters use this technique to create an illusion of reality – a landscape glimpsed through a 'doorway', or a 'fireplace' on a wall, effects which are beyond the scope of amateurs. What is possible is to create small details by tracing a design (like a jug of flowers or plates on a shelf, for example) on to a wall or cupboard and then filling it in. Don't attempt to achieve a realistic effect; aim for one that's joky and will still be fun in six months' time.

Murals are wall paintings which can be built up piece by piece using a grid. Draw a grid over the design to be copied and then a similar but large-scale grid on the wall. The design is transferred one square (and colour) at a time. If you are decorating the playroom with a zoo mural, for example, look at the square showing the giraffe's neck and copy that on to the wall before proceeding to the next square which shows the ears and the head. When the mural is complete, rub out the guidelines with a damp cloth and outline the whole with felt tip if you think it needs more emphasis, but remember this may make it more difficult to cover.

FACESAVERS

● Affix temporary friezes (such as short-life nursery designs) on to painted walls with double-sided tape.

● When you have completed the first stencil, reverse the card to form a flowing pattern. Remember to clean the stencil first!

● Improvise with potato prints, pastry cutters or set squares to create an impromptu border.

● Look for wallpaper designs which can be used as stripes or cut to form a border.

● Enlarge a motif from a border to form a large stencil for decorating the centre of cupboard doors or occasional tables.

● Cover unattractive wallpaper with plain or stippled-effect paper panels in co-ordinating colours as a temporary measure.

● Create an easy-clean dado to disguise grubby but sound wallpaper by painting the lower third of the wall and covering the join (seam) with a patterned paper frieze.

● Use plain fabric which co-ordinates with patterned curtains to make a pelmet (valance), frill and matching tie-backs to give standard drapes a traditional look.

● Paint a striped border on a plain roller blind and sew matching ribbon on to towels to add style to a small bathroom.

A mural need not be on a wall to have impact. This delicate panel design of Noah's ark and the animals transforms a previously blank area into the room's focal point.

CHAPTER 8

On the level

Nothing receives quite as much abuse as the floor of your home. Dirt is walked on to it, grit is ground into it and heaven knows what's spilled on it. Yet more often than not we insist on covering it with carpet to give warmth and comfort, a treatment which would have amazed our ancestors, who believed that carpets were for hanging on walls.

Although modern fibres and techniques make it possible to use carpet virtually everywhere, from the stairs (where it is subject to greatest wear), to bathrooms (where it must contend with damp) and kitchens (where non-woven carpet tiles will shrug off the occasional broken egg), it's worth considering the alternatives. In every home there will be a subfloor of floorboards, plywood or chipboard which could be exposed to make an attractive and inexpensive floor or covered with wood strip, mosaic or parquet. Think about ceramic tiles or quarries (the unglazed equivalent), resilient rubber, vinyl or cork tiles, or easy-care sheet flooring. If you're lucky enough to have a brick or flagstone floor, you'll need to maintain the finish – and if you're stuck with concrete there's always floor paint.

What if you're determined to have carpet? Provided you choose the right grade for each area of wear you can use it with confidence throughout the house. Don't overlook the contribution that rugs and runners can make to the decor, and remember carpet's original role as a work of art. Hand-made Oriental carpets are an investment that always appreciates, while many of the rugs and squares produced by craftsmen in the West resemble abstract paintings or soft sculpture.

SUBFLOORS

How can you complete a room if you can't afford flooring? Perhaps you have moved into a house bought on a large mortgage and the budget simply won't stretch to more than basic furnishings – or perhaps you dislike the existing carpet or floorcovering but can't afford to replace it with the quality required.

The answer is to examine the subfloor. You may be lucky enough to find attractive quarry tiles or woodblock hidden beneath shabby carpet or sheet flooring, though frankly you're more likely to find concrete or floorboards. But whether it's made from floorboards, chipboard or even concrete, the

Flooring plays an important part in a room which relies on texture rather than colour or pattern for effect. Warm woodblock offsets the cream walls and glass shelves in the foreground while pale carpet contrasts with the dramatic background beyond.

subfloor can often be varnished, stained or painted to create an attractive topfloor – and after all, it's there for free.

WOOD AND BOARD

Both traditional boards and the sheets of chipboard often used as a subfloor in modern homes can be coloured and varnished, provided the following conditions are fulfilled.

The subfloor is in good repair.

If only a few boards are broken it may be worth replacing them, but if a large number have been cut for access to pipes and wiring or are splintered, the floor will never repay your hard work. Examine the floor carefully for sagging boards or panels (which should be secured) and for signs of woodworm or rot, which need immediate professional attention. Gaps between boards may also pose problems. Narrow gaps can be plugged with fillets of wood or papier mâché but boards which are more than about 1/8 inch (3 mm) apart should be relaid – you will find this a tricky job which is rarely worth doing purely for the sake of appearance.

The subfloor is made of good-quality materials.

This means hardwood (only found in a few period homes), substantial softwood boards, high-quality chipboard, or plywood. It's a crime to cover hardwood boards, so go ahead and treat them unless they are in very poor condition. Standard floorboards pose the greatest problems because the quality varies greatly. As a rule of thumb, old houses tend to have thicker boards than new ones because the builders were more lavish with timber. On the other hand they may be affected by rot or woodworm. As a general rule, don't try to sand boards which are thin or splinter easily.

The colour is uniform.

It doesn't matter if the entire subfloor has been stained, but if only part has been coloured it may be impossible to remove all the stain by sanding. You will need to apply wood bleach to the area to achieve an even colour, and as it can be a tricky process it's worth testing the technique on a patch of floor before you commit yourself.

SANDING, COLOURING AND SEALING

This is a cheap and effective method of transforming plain boards into a floor to be proud of, but be

Blue and white vinyl 'tiles' – painted boards, in fact – create a cheery, informal atmosphere for a family dining room, complemented by café-style bentwood chairs, and primrose-painted walls and window frames with matching Venetian blinds.

warned – it involves work that's heavy and dirty as well as hard. Protective clothing (ear protectors, goggles and a face mask) is a must when using a powered sander and you'll need a cool, airy environment when using varnish because of the high amount of solvent it contains.

Sanding floorboards needs careful preparation before you can start. First tap down all protruding nail heads and countersunk screws. (It's well worth using a pipe and cable detector device to avoid the risk of puncturing pipe runs.) Fill the gaps with wedge-shaped slivers of wood or papier mâché coloured to blend with the boards, and plane smooth. For sanding you'll need to hire (rent) a power sander with dust bag. These are efficient but extremely heavy and tiring to use, so don't underestimate the length of time the work will take. Run it diagonally across the boards first, using coarse abrasive to remove inground varnish and grime, then fit medium-grade abrasive and sand the boards along the grain. Finally, sand along the grain once more using fine abrasive. Remember to keep the sander on the move and to switch it off before you turn round on reaching a wall or you will gouge the floorboards. The last step is to sand the areas where the power sander cannot reach, using a belt or an orbital

sander and working along the grain.

Colouring comes next. Try to obtain as even a colour as possible.

To lighten wood it's best to use wood bleach (though domestic bleach will do) and rinse well. Sand lightly if the process raises the wood grain.

Wood dye adds colour. It is dissolved in water, which penetrates quickly but may raise the grain, or alcohol, which dries fast – sometimes too fast for even colour. Bright colours in place of the traditional wood shades can be very effective. A deep green floor, for example, would look stylish in a dining room furnished with cane furniture and lace curtains, while scarlet or yellow could brighten up a playroom and grey-blue or rose might suit a sitting room. Combine colours by dyeing selected boards to form stripes but take care that the colour doesn't bleed, or the whole effect will be spoiled.

Wood stains are usually solvent-based liquids and gels which are available in a more restricted range of effects. They produce a sheen but take time to dry and must not be applied too thickly.

Colour-washing and colour-rubbing are two traditional techniques. In colour-washing thinned emulsion (latex paint) is brushed along the grain; with colour-rubbing, emulsion (latex) or eggshell (alkyd semigloss) is brushed into the grain and then rubbed off for subtle colour. Ivory and grey, the classic colours for floors, are particularly effective for toning down the colour of new floorboards but pastels also look pretty, especially in bedrooms.

Paint, whether emulsion (latex), eggshell (alkyd semigloss), gloss or undercoat (which has an attractive chalky appearance), is another possibility. As it conceals the grain of the wood, it's not necessary to take much trouble to sand the boards – the usual light sanding before priming and painting woodwork will do. Paint also gives more scope for creating pattern as it will obscure individual boards. You could divide the floor into squares and add diamonds at corners for a fake marble tile effect, or use a painted floor as a base for stencilling (also effective on colour-washed or rubbed boards).

All these treatments need protecting with at least three coats of heavy-duty varnish, but you can short-circuit the process by protecting and tinting in one using coloured varnish. A wide range of colours is available, but the disadvantages are that it can be tricky to predict the precise shade and that the colour will chip if the varnish does, making areas of wear more apparent.

Sealing completes the process. The surface of the

floor must be completely clean and free from grease and dust before you apply varnish. This isn't the only seal you can use but it is the most hard-wearing. You may prefer the softer sheen of wax polish, but remember that it demands more effort to maintain. (Synthetic varnish is simply swept and damp-mopped.) Clear polyurethane varnish is probably the most versatile and hardwearing product. Make sure you choose a type that's suitable for floors, because some matt (flat) effect varnishes are for decorative use only. Gloss, satin or semi-gloss are usually suitable, as are yacht varnish and cold-cure (epoxy) varnish, where two ingredients are mixed to form a tough but very shiny finish. Dilute the first coat of varnish with 10 per cent white spirit and brush it along the grain. Subsequent coats (at least three) should be applied at 24-hour intervals. You'll need to sand lightly and wipe clean between each one, and it's worth adding a dash of white gloss to the varnish to prevent yellowing.

TREATING BOARD

Hardboard is a subfloor used to give stability to sheet flooring or tiles. It's laid rough side up so the texture will show through even when it is painted. Don't use it in areas of hard wear, nor in rooms where it is likely to get wet because it will swell in the damp.

Chipboard is available in several grades. Good quality chipboard will make a satisfactory topfloor provided it's not exposed to damp – so don't use it in kitchens or bathrooms. Seal with polyurethane varnish or with cork floor seal, which is particularly suitable for porous surfaces.

Plywood is made from layers of wood bonded carefully together to create a strong and stable material suitable for flooring. It makes an effective topfloor, whether it's a restored subfloor or bought new and laid over floorboards; cut it into tiles, using a circular saw for the best effect.

Any of the colouring treatments used for floorboards can be used on man-made board too. Because you are not limited by the pattern floorboards impose, it's easier to create a tiled effect or to form abstract patterns. Experiment with combing, where a rubber, wood or even cardboard comb is run through wet paint to form a wavy pattern; stippling, where a topcoat of paint is dabbed with a stubby brush (you can improvise with a shoe brush); or, for the adventurous, imitation marbling. Remember to protect any treatment with floor quality polyurethane varnish.

CONCRETE

Basements, conservatories, utility rooms and kitchens are the places where you are most likely to find a concrete floor. Brighten it up with hardwearing floor paint, similar to that used in factories. It is suitable for wood as well as concrete, and though the colour range isn't adventurous you'll find green, red, black, white and blue, which will blend with most settings and give plenty of scope for inventive decoration.

SMOOTH FLOORS

Installing most permanent floorings is a major operation but there are some materials which can be laid over existing floorings for a quick cover-up. All flooring, however, needs a stable sub-floor, which means hardboard laid rough side up over floorboards or a level solid floor that's free from damp. Cork and vinyl tiles and vinyl sheet and cushioned flooring can sometimes be laid over ceramic or quarry tiles which have been rubbed with wire (steel) wool to give a 'key' for the adhesive but check before you buy, as a latex self-levelling compound which forms an even barrier may be recommended. It's usually necessary to take up old linoleum and vinyl (tiles and sheet)

Sanded and sealed floorboards have a classic, country-style appeal. Protect the surface with several coats of matt (flat)-finish varnish, which simulates wax polish and needs the minimum of care.

Above: Clay tiles in a Provençal shape suit crisp modern rooms as well as rustic settings, as this kitchen shows. Mix the tiles well when laying these or conventional quarries, as the depth of colour will vary from batch to batch.

Far right: Choose profile-design rubber or vinyl flooring for high-tech interiors. This charcoal-coloured floor will resist wear and is impervious to water; it's also a practical colour, as raised designs can be difficult to clean.

before laying new sheet flooring, but you could try covering *smooth* floorings with unwaxed brown paper first.

Be creative with flooring by laying vinyl tiles in a border effect or by combining rectangles of sheet flooring in different colours to form an abstract design. Many tiles are easy to lay. Consider white, coloured or natural cork tiles for resilience and warmth, wood mosaic squares for traditional elegance, lino tiles (still found in the UK, often in softer colours than vinyl) for a sophisticated or classical setting, and rubber for a hardwearing 'high-tech' floor. If you prefer sheet or cushioned vinyl, choose a design to emphasize the room's style. A wide range is available, from traditional tile designs to up-to-the-minute grids, spatter and speckled effects. Widths are usually 6 ft 6 in, 9 ft 9 in or 13 ft (2, 3 and 4 m) – 6 ft or 12 ft in America – to avoid the need for seams, but wide flooring can be unwieldy.

CARPET

Adapting carpet is often a matter of seeing it in a new light. The floral Axminster which fights with

your sofas may look fine with the plain walls and windows in a bedroom, and a carpet that's frayed at the edges can be relaid to suit a smaller room.

Beware of false economies: will the carpet last long enough, and look good enough, to justify the cost of fitting and new underlay (padding)? Don't try to use bedroom carpet downstairs unless you are sure it is suitable for general domestic use and avoid using remnants of wool carpet in the bathroom where it may rot. On the other hand, don't throw carpet away unless you are sure that it cannot be put to any other use. For example, you could combine the best part of two carpets of similar construction using special adhesive tape to create a bordered square or an abstract design, mitring the corners for a professional finish. Dyeing is not recommended because, as it's impossible to immerse the carpet, you can't guarantee an even finish.

RUGS

An alternative to moving or replacing carpet is to cover it with a runner or rug. Rugs will do more than conceal a pattern you dislike; they can also be used to relate the floor to other patterns and colours which feature in the room scheme.

Many people choose a neutral colour for fitted (wall-to-wall) carpet so that it will adapt to a number of schemes, but sometimes the floor needs more emphasis. Some lines of furnishings now include co-ordinating rugs and dhurries so you can be sure that colours and designs will blend, and your colour board (see page 16) will be invaluable when choosing a rug to suit other schemes.

A rug can also be used for definition. Placed in the centre of a seating group or beneath a dining table, it will bring the area sharply into focus. Remember to use a rug that's large enough for effect and choose patterns and colours which contribute to the scheme. Always opt for one large rug rather than a clutter of small ones. If you want to protect the carpet in front of the sofas, where it wears most, as well as by the fire, choose one large square rather than two separate rugs. Use plain rugs on patterned carpet or in rooms with boldly patterned wallpaper. Many rugs with distinctive patterns and lovely colours deserve to be a focal point of the room, but unless they mix well with your existing furnishings they should form the starting point of a new scheme instead.

For safety, never place rugs on polished floors or near doorways where people may trip. Fit anti-creep fibre to the reverse side to prevent rugs from

Above: A ceramic tiled floor with a marble effect is an appropriate and a romantic choice for this lovely conservatory, where voile drapes are used in place of shutters to screen the light.

Right: Traditional or modern, Oriental carpets have the abstract pattern and attention to detail which give interest to a simple scheme. Here the colours are restricted to dark blue and white to complement the plain walls and transparent drapes.

moving on carpet or choose vinyl-coated netting underlay for use on smooth floors.

WHAT'S IN A NAME?

Carpets and rugs come in a vast array of types and there is sure to be one to suit your interior. From traditional Axminsters to ethnic rugs from India and Greece – the choice is almost endless.

Axminster carpets and rugs have a woven backing and a pattern formed by a cut pile. They are often traditional in design, though modern geometrics are also available.

Brussels weave rugs are plain or patterned with a dense looped pile.

Chenille rugs are made from cotton with a nubbly pile. They are usually washable, so are suitable for bathrooms, but are for light wear only.

Chinese carpets combine different heights of wool pile to create the distinctive sculpted motifs which include flowers (to represent the seasons) as well as the dragon, phoenix, lion and dog (religious and political figures). The soft colours are also emblematic – jade green, rose pink, blue and cream shades are popular.

Coir (or coconut fibre) matting is made from coconut fibre woven in a herringbone design. It may be latex (rubber)-backed to prevent curl. It's an attractive and hardwearing floorcovering but it is no longer cheap and can be difficult to clean. The latex (rubber)-backed varieties are more suitable for kitchens and bathrooms than the unbacked type.

Dhurries come from India. They are fringed rugs made from cotton or cotton and wool, often hand-woven in ethnic or geometric designs and pastel colours. They are sometimes reversible. Colours may bleed, so place lining paper beneath the dhurry if it is used over carpet. They are really only suitable for light wear.

Flokati rugs are from Greece. They have a very long wool pile, and are usually white or dark brown. They are for light wear.

Indian carpets are plain wool carpets (cream is the classic colour) with fringes and a dense pile.

Numdahs or namdas are small felt rugs in cheerful ethnic designs in soft or bright colours on a cream ground. They are for light wear only.

Rag rugs are made from multi-coloured scraps of cotton woven in a striped effect. They are suitable for light wear only.

Runners are long narrow strips of carpet or coir used to protect flooring in halls and walkways.

Rush mats are stitched together from individual

Wall-to-wall carpet makes the most of limited space, especially if you choose a colour to co-ordinate with the walls, as here. The velvet pile can be created by a classic Wilton weave/ wool combination or by the tufting process using synthetic fibres.

'bullseye' squares. They look right in a cottage setting but tend to fray, so they are not suitable for heavy use.

Sisal is made from the leaves of a tropical plant. It is hard-wearing but slippery (so not for use on stairs) and, like coir, is easier to care for when latex (rubber)-backed.

Wilton weave carpets have lengths of yarn woven into the backing to form a hardwearing carpet with a dense velvet pile. Wilton rugs are often patterned (up to five colours can be used) in contrast to fitted Wilton carpet, which is usually plain.

ORIENTAL CARPETS

Oriental carpets are hand-knotted in symbolic patterns and rich colours. They come from Iran (which used to be called Persia), Pakistan, Turkey and parts of the USSR. Antique designs are museum pieces but traditional patterns are still produced today, mainly by co-operative workshops.

Persian carpets were the finest Oriental carpets. Traditionally they had a silk or fine wool pile with flower, tree, animal or medallion motifs.

Turkish carpets differ from Persian because by tradition they have abstract designs. Colours and patterns vary according to the area where they are produced.

Khilims or kelims are brightly coloured Oriental tapestry rugs.

Prayer rugs are the mats on which Moslems pray. The design shows part of the mosque.

FACESAVERS

• Use fabric dye if you are aiming for a watery colour effect on floorboards.

• Broadloom carpet can sometimes be supplied as a room-sized rug with finished sides and fringed ends – a better choice than fitted (wall-to-wall) carpet if you intend to move house.

• Stencil a border on to floorboards to co-ordinate with soft furnishings, giving a professional finish.

• Turn rugs and carpet squares regularly to minimize wear.

• Lay sheet flooring over unwaxed brown paper if you can't take up a smooth subfloor.

• Use a white rug or an Indian carpet over dark flooring if a room is rather gloomy to make the most of restricted natural light.

• Cover a worn hall carpet with a smart runner.

• Lay carpet over wood or tiles to improve insulation and reduce noise levels. Take pity on neighbours if you live in a flat or apartment above ground floor level.

CHAPTER 9

All wrapped up

Fabric is too useful to be confined to curtains. Use it by the yard to drape walls, tent a ceiling or create a fantasy headboard, or turn it into cushions, chair covers and topcloths (slipcovers). If you are not handy with a sewing machine then don't neglect textiles which come ready-made – quilts, duvet or comforter covers and bed and table linen are just as effective in providing that finishing touch.

BEDTIME STORY
Colourful, attractive bedlinen has been one of the furnishing industry's recent success stories. In the UK its introduction coincided with the arrival of the duvet, or continental quilt, that bag of down, feathers, polyester or even wool which revolutionizes bedmaking because it precludes top sheets (no tucking in or hospital corners) and gives warmth without the weight of blankets or ordinary quilts. Sheets, blankets and comforters continue to be popular in the USA, while in the UK variations on the duvet theme have produced the seasonal duvet which separates into sections as the weather demands, the 'comforter' or padded top quilt and the electric duvet for the ultimate in warmth.

STYLES
A change of colour scheme often involves a change of bedding and there's plenty from which to choose. Many ranges of co-ordinates include bedlinen with companion curtains, wallpapers, sheers, borders, paint and accessories like table lamps and bedside rugs. They may repeat the pattern of curtains or blinds or this may be adapted to form a panelled design.

Florals are top favourite, ranging from stylized modern designs in unusual colour combinations to traditional prints. In contrast, plain white and ivory are also popular, uniform in colour but ruffled and embroidered like a Victorian night gown. Also available are abstract designs in brilliant colours, 'masculine' styles in deep navy and burgundy, plain pastels and primaries, and a host of nursery designs. Alongside the fashionable styles are classic cotton or flannelette sheets to use with wool or acrylic blankets.

BLANKETS VERSUS DUVETS
Comfort is a matter of taste. Sheets and blankets tuck in securely but may leave draughty gaps at the top. Blankets are usually heavier than duvets because they are made from wool, acrylic or a blend of fibres. A duvet moulds itself to your contours, but natural fillings need shaking up regularly. Duvets are light because they are filled with down or feathers from waterfowl – not chickens – or polyester. (The few which contain wool or silk and wool are more weighty.) Goose down has the best warmth-to-weight ratio, followed by duck down, down and feather (more down than feather) and feather and down. Polyester filling is either continuous or cut into short pieces (staple fibres) to simulate the 'loft' provided by feathers or down.

Warmth is not just a personal matter. It can actually be measured by units called togs. In the UK there is a specific standard for duvets because unlike blankets, which are used together, the duvet is used alone, apart from its protective cover. The tog rating for duvets runs from 4.5 (summer use and similar to the warmth provided by two blankets and a bedspread) to 13.5 (for extra warmth). Most people like a duvet of around 10 togs, but there's a trend towards warmer 11 or 12 tog duvets made from duck down or improved polyester. Duvets like these are among the most expensive, not only because the filling is costly but because the case construction is more complicated to prevent cold spots where the channels are stitched. The warmth of comforters purchased in the US can be judged by loft; the higher the loft, the warmer the comforter.

Durability is where blankets score better than duvets. Duvets should be replaced after 10 years as the filling (especially feathers) breaks up with wear. You should never crush or compress a duvet so they are not ideal for bedsits (studio apartments), and even washable duvets are only supposed to be laundered infrequently.

Convenience is important and there's no doubt that duvets simplify bedmaking, especially in bunks. Team with a fitted sheet so all that's needed is to plump up the filling every morning.

Style needs some consideration. Although there are duvet covers in designs to suit all settings, they may look too casual for a formal or traditional room. Because you shouldn't top a duvet with anything but its cover, you can't use conventional quilts or fitted bedspreads (though a lace bedcover won't make

Diaphanous fabric swathed over ceiling-mounted curtain poles will create a tester-bed effect, used at the head of the bed, or a fake four-poster if separate lengths are draped along each side.

much difference). Sheets and blankets, on the other hand, have a neat appearance that's the ideal base for quilts and bedspreads of all kinds.

Cost is little different if you compare similar qualities. Egyptian cotton sheets and merino wool blankets will equal the price of a goose down duvet at one end of the price scale while cotton blend sheets and acrylic blankets will cost roughly the same as a polyester-filled duvet at the other. There are a few hidden costs to consider. You're likely to need two duvet covers with matching pillowcases (one to wash and one to wear) plus a valance (dust ruffle), or valanced bottom sheets, to hide the bed base. Weigh that against the price of a change of sheets and a bedspread for use with blankets when assessing the difference in cost.

THEME FOR A DREAM

Do you want a romantic retreat or a modern bedroom decorated in bright colours and strong graphic designs? Does the room double as a playroom, study or bedsit (studio)? Do you want a telephone and a television or to get away from them?

These questions need answering before you choose bedlinen if you want a successful scheme.

Pretty private means you can turn bedroom into boudoir by the lavish use of ruffles, ribbon and lace in pastels, white or cream. Make the bed the centrepiece of the room by draping it with fabric to resemble a four-poster. There are several ways of doing this, but most rely on suspending rods or curtain poles from the ceiling. Use conventional curtain poles hung on chains at the foot and head of the bed and drape with lace bedspreads – just the

Chintzy cottons give a crisp look. Here, a pretty floral print is used for a co-ordinating tablecloth, valance and curtains, complete with swags and tails. Heaped cushions and pillows and a casually draped shawl soften the effect.

BED AND BEDDING SIZES (UK)			
BED SIZES			
Singles		30 × 75 in	75 × 190 cm
		36 × 75 in	90 × 190 cm
		39 × 78 in	100 × 200 cm
Doubles		54 × 75 in	135 × 190 cm
		60 × 78 in	150 × 200 cm
Bedding sizes/duvets			
To fit bed size		36 × 75 in	90 × 190 cm
Single duvet		53 × 79 in	135 × 200 cm
To fit bed size		39 × 78 in	100 × 200 cm
Extra-long single duvet		53 × 87 in	135 × 220 cm
To fit bed size		54 × 75 in	135 × 190 cm
Double duvet		79 × 79 in	200 × 200 cm
To fit bed size		54 × 75 in	135 × 190 cm
Extra long double duvet		79 × 87 in	200 × 220 cm
To fit bed size		60 × 78 in	150 × 200 cm
King size duvet		89 × 87 in	225 × 220 cm
Bedding sizes/sheets			
To fit bed size		36 × 75 in	90 × 190 cm
Flat sheet		69 × 101 in	175 × 255 cm
To fit bed size		54 × 75 in	135 × 190 cm
Flat sheet		89 × 100 in	225 × 255 cm
To fit bed size		60 × 78 in	150 × 200 cm
Flat sheet		108 × 116 in	275 × 295 cm

Flat sheets vary in size; these sizes are the most popular

For fitted sheets *see* bed sizes

right width. Loop the fabric into swags and pin it in place or use satin ribbon tied into bows. Choose a pretty pastel or white cover beneath and heap the top of the bed with cushions and pillows which bring together the colours in the scheme. Alternatively, use the curtains at the window to frame the bed. Provided it's not draughty you can use lace curtains or cotton, chintz or imitation silk drapes tied back on each side of the bed during the day and drawn to cover the window at night. The wide-width polyester/cotton sold by the yard or metre for bedlinen, striped sheets or gingham will substitute for lace if you prefer – sew a pinch or pencil heading to hang from curtain rings for precision. Keep to light fabrics which drape well.

If you are on a tight budget, paint plastic pipes and

BED AND BEDDING SIZES (US)

Mattress sizes

Twin		39 × 75 in	99 × 190 cm
Full		54 × 75 in	137 × 190 cm
Queen		60 × 80 in	153 × 203 cm
King		78 × 80 in	198 × 203 cm
	or	72 × 84 in	182 × 213 cm

Bedding sizes/comforters

To fit twin bed size		39 × 75 in	99 × 190 cm
Comforter		68 × 86 in	173 × 218 cm
To fit full bed size		54 × 75 in	137 × 190 cm
Comforter		86 × 86 in	218 × 218 cm
To fit queen bed size		60 × 80 in	152 × 203 cm
Comforter		86 × 86 in	218 × 218 cm
To fit king bed size		78 × 80 in	198 × 203 cm
	or	72 × 84 in	182 × 213 cm
Comforter		100 × 90 in	254 × 229 cm

Bedding sizes/sheets

To fit twin bed size		39 × 75 in	99 × 190 cm
Sheets (flat)		66 × 96 in	167 × 243 cm
To fit full bed size		54 × 75 in	137 × 190 cm
Sheets (flat)		81 × 96 in	205 × 243 cm
To fit queen bed size		60 × 80 in	152 × 203 cm
Sheets (flat)		90 × 102 in	228 × 259 cm
To fit king bed size		78 × 80 in	198 × 203 cm
	or	72 × 84 in	182 × 213 cm
Sheets (flat)		108 × 102 in	274 × 259 cm

Note: Duvets are not generally available in the US

joints a bright colour and join them to follow the shape of the bed. Hang them from the ceiling by fine chains and drape lengths of cheesecloth at each corner so that it falls in pools on the floor. Make a Roman blind the same colour as the pipes for a small window or use more cheesecloth at large ones and add neutral or white bedding for a cool modern look which won't overstretch your finances.

If a four-poster seems excessive, consider copying a tester bed, which has curtains at the head. Fit curved curtain track to the ceiling above the pillow area and add a frilly valance (pelmet) to hide it. Hang ruffled, fully lined curtains from the track (secure them with tie-backs or ribbon if you like) and let plain lining fabric cascade down the back. You could also fix a large hook into the ceiling and wind sheer fabric around it so that the drapes fall loosely on each side; fill up the background with a fall of cheesecloth or lace. Don't forget details like ribbons, rosettes, corded or piped tie-backs and tassels, but remember that whatever you choose should be in keeping with the room's style and the colour scheme. Remember too that these drapes are not for children, who'll be tempted to swing on them, nor for industrial areas where they will soil quickly, nor for *anyone* who smokes in bed.

Graphic art is for men who have been known to object to the wholesale takeover of the 'master' bedroom by feminine schemes – and simpler styles often suit dual-purpose and teenagers' bedrooms too. Add interest to the bed by using a Venetian or miniblind, mirror or lattice screen (improvise with

Length means luxury where draping is concerned – and that's true of bedspreads and bedlinen, as well as curtains. Let fabrics flow on to the floor for a sumptuous look, effective even with budget-price materials.

garden trellis) at the foot or by placing the bed in an unusual position – it doesn't have to go against a wall. If there's room, try placing it back to back with a trestle table which doubles as a desk to separate sleeping and study areas, or against the back of a wardrobe or chest to create a dressing 'room'. Use blinds or simple curtains, caught up at the corners for diagonal emphasis, at the windows.

Junior choice caters for children's particular needs. Don't use decorative drapes in children's rooms. They'll swing on them, pull them down and may even strangle themselves. If your daughter yearns for Little Princess-style frills, create a 'coronet' on the ceiling with looped side pieces secured to the wall well out of reach. Provide a pretty duvet cover to co-ordinate with curtains, a lacy bedspread or a special quilt and add plenty of ruffled cushions as accessories. Boys and girls both appreciate a graphic scheme, while younger children like bright primary and secondary colours.

There's a wealth of attractive bedding for young children and as long as you choose basic furnishings which will adapt to their changing taste and needs,

it's worth adding bedlinen and blinds in bright nursery designs to which children can relate.

LOOSE LIVING

Drapes are as effective in the living room as in the bedroom. Though they're most popular as window treatments, whether used alone or to form a frame for conventional curtains or blinds, lengths of fabric are also ideal for pinning to walls, draping from ceilings, or covering furniture that's seen better days.

Tented ceilings can't fail to impress. They're best for dining rooms, bedrooms and even bathrooms where you don't stay long enough to tire of the effect; all you need is plenty of fabric and a staple gun. In a small room, drape the fabric from a circle of hooks in the centre and allow it to billow on to the walls. It can be stapled direct to plasterboard walls or to battens (slats).

In a large room, secure the swathes by cords or fine poles which run from side to side to create a wave effect. If you want to paint or paper the walls you'll need to finish the fabric neatly at cornice or picture rail level and hide the join with a moulding or frieze. Alternatively you can opt for …

Fabric-covered walls, the natural companions for a tented ceiling. The fabric can be pleated, loosely draped or stretched by battens (slats) at floor and ceiling level. It's an effective way of hiding poor plaster and improving acoustics but expensive, so choose budget-price fabric like striped mattress ticking (smart but heavy), wide-width poly/cotton or curtain lining. Draping sheer muslin over richly coloured walls will create a translucent effect at minimal cost. Accessories should be in proportion; add deeply scalloped swags and fringes, tassels and large bows. Don't be tempted to economize on fabric. When draping material, nothing succeeds like excess! A look like this won't last forever as the fabric will fade in the folds and will be difficult to clean. Use a vacuum cleaner on minimum suction to clean the drapes and reverse the airflow to blow dust from swags and folds from time to time, to keep things looking fresh.

CUSHY NUMBERS

Cushions add more than comfort to a room. They provide an ideal opportunity for co-ordination because they can bring together colours and patterns used elsewhere in the room. An easy way to co-ordinate is to use cushions which match curtains or the upholstery and to add other cushions in pat-

Mass cushions on a sofa, bed or window seat, choosing colours and fabrics which relate to the room scheme. Contrast piping emphasizes the style, whether the cushion is large, like the one forming the window seat, or small, like those on top.

terns or colours which blend with both. A traditional room needs tapestry, ruffled and quilted designs, or feature cushions – an old lace pillow, appliqué cushion or a design painted on silk – to give the collection a lift; you can never have too many scatter cushions. Modern settings need a bolder touch with square cushions in abstract patterns, strong colours and minimal trim.

Plain cushion covers are easy to make because they are simply an envelope of fabric. Fit a zipper for a snug fit and easy removal. (Velcro will substitute if your sewing skills are shaky.) It's worth hoarding scraps of fabric for appliqué and patchwork designs. Remember that crafts like these don't need to be in traditional style; attach a big bow or a chequered border to a plain cushion for an uncompromisingly modern look and embroider faces and animals on nursery cushions, avoiding long hair or tails which could be swallowed. Feather and foam-filled cushion pads come in all shapes and sizes: pillows and hearts for a romantic bedroom, large Ottoman squares and scatter cushions for the living room, neck pillows for the bathroom. They will replace furniture too. Make sag bags (bean bags) filled with polystyrene beads or large floor cushions to use with a frame for cheap and colourful seating, or make a piped box cushion to co-ordinate with curtains for use on a toy chest or window seat. Make sure that you opt for tough upholstery fabrics (tightly woven cotton, linen union or acrylic velvet) which will resist wear when planning substitute seating like this.

LOOSE COVERS

These can be made in colours and fabrics which are impractical for fixed upholstery, though you'll still need to choose durable, and preferably washable, materials. Use them to extend the life of your furniture, to change the decor or give a seasonal emphasis (you could have patterned covers for summer and plain for winter, for example) or to renovate sofas and chairs which are past their best, but which can't be replaced yet.

There's a wider choice of fabrics for loose covers than for fixed upholstery because they are not under constant tension and wear is distributed more evenly. Look at tightly woven acrylic and cotton (allow for shrinkage or wash the material before it is made up) or linen union. Cover seam edges with piping to blend or contrast, make arm-caps to take the brunt of soiling and wear and choose a valance (box-pleated, frilled or straight) to suit the style of

the room and furniture.

Loose covers complement modern as well as classic furniture. Copy the fashionable 'duvet' style seating which has a top quilt with a removable cover to give new life to a tired sofa; alternatively consider a throw to add interest.

Floral loose covers have a cottagey charm. Here they are partnered by simple, over-length drapes with an interesting quilted finish.

Right: A cover-cum-throw stitched in simple envelope shapes combines the appeal of drapes with the practicality of a loose cover. Matching white curtains are turned over at the top to make a casual modern pelmet (valance).

Far right: Rescue a sofa that's seen better days by draping it with a colourful bedcover or a double width of furnishing fabric. Pile high with plain and patterned cushions and give it importance with a backdrop of co-ordinating material.

THROWS

It's not only windows which can be draped; sofas and armchairs can look equally effective swathed in fabric. There are several methods. Throws which have the prosaic purpose of covering worn covers or protecting new ones will need to be fixed firmly in place, while more elaborate drapes are frankly for decoration only. Although you can improvise with sheeting or lengths of fabric, the best throws are made from material which clings, like fine wool (the best choice but expensive), acrylic or thick polyester. Brighten up a dull armchair by trailing a large wool challis or polyester shawl (fringed if possible) over the arm and back or drape a fine rug or blanket over a sofa. Place the throw asymmetrically and let it fall into folds. Colours and patterns should relate to your colour scheme but there's no need for strict co-ordination; the idea is to mingle different textiles for effect. For a more practical cover-up, use a large purpose-made throw firmly tucked in and securely anchored by tasselled cord wrapped round the base of the chair or sofa.

Turn a basic plywood table into a piece to be proud of by covering it with a floor-length tablecloth. Choose colours to blend with the room scheme, as this honey-coloured cloth does.

TABLE TALK

What's your idea of a tablecloth? Sumptuous linen or lace over a mahogany table? Floor-length drapes over a circular side table? Or brightly coloured PVC (vinyl) covering the family dining table to withstand spills from fruit juice or paint?

Tablecloths can be any of these. They may form a permanent part of the room scheme, covering a shabby dining table or a chipboard occasional table. They may be used for formal dinners or just at family meals.

Damask is a figured fabric used for classic white tablecloths. Linen is the fibre traditionally used for damask cloths, but heavy cotton may substitute. Both fibres should be washed at a high temperature and starched if necessary. Use damask in formal settings with crystal glass, cobalt or gold-rimmed bone china and silver cutlery.

Embroidered tablecloths should be washed with care as the dyes may bleed. These lovely cloths usually have delicate traditional designs and look best with place settings similar to those for lace.

Lace tablecloths are made from cotton or polyester. They too suit a traditional setting. Use them over a plain white cloth for elegance or over a deep or pastel coloured cloth to co-ordinate with the decor and team with patterned china, fine glass and decorative cutlery.

Plain tablecloths are made from cotton, cotton blends, polyester, or acrylic for cloths which are cosy rather than crisp. Look for cloths with contrast-piped edging, lace inserts or a fringe for interest. Use with plain china or tableware in traditional or graphic designs, plain glass and cutlery and napkins in contrasting plain colours.

Printed tablecloths are usually made from cotton or a polyester/cotton blend. Pure polyester is also used but it may look limp. Look at border patterns which show off the shape of the table and choose a design which relates to furnishings first, tableware second. Use with plain, co-ordinating or border-printed fine china or earthenware, with plain napkins, plain glass and stainless steel cutlery.

PVC (vinyl) fabric makes a cheerful, water-resistant table-covering. Look at Art Nouveau designs for a country kitchen, bright geometrics for modern appeal, or a washable acrylic cloth with a waterproof backing for a softer, more conventional look. Use pottery mugs and stoneware with country-kitchen designs, bright earthenware or plastic, and cutlery with coloured plastic handles to go with bold colours and designs.

SIZES

Tablecloths should overhang the table by at least 6 inches (15 cm), more for formal cloths (even to floor-length if wanted). Popular sizes are as follows:

Square 54 inches (137 cm) square. Seats 4.
Oblong 54 × 72 inches (137 × 183 cm). Seats 4-6.
        54 × 90 inches (137 by 229 cm). Seats 6-8.
Round 72 inches (183 cm) diameter. Seats 6.
Oval 72 × 90 inches (183 × 229 cm). Seats 6-8.
Napkins 10 to 20 inches (25 to 50 cm) square.

CRAFTY IDEAS

Make a circular tablecloth for a round dining table, or co-ordinating top and bottom cloths for a round occasional table. To avoid a central seam, fold the fabric into quarters wrong side out. Cut a piece of string the same length as the side of the square and tie a pencil to it. Now pin the string to the folded corner and draw a line from one edge to the other to create a quarter-circle. Cut along the line and open out your circular cloth.

Make placemats or a cutlery roll – informal place mats with loops to hold cutlery, which are ideal for a buffet party or picnic as they can be rolled up and secured neatly. Simply trim rectangles of quilted fabric with bias binding for a place-mat and add loops for cutlery and napkins for a cutlery roll. Finish with a tie to secure the roll.

Tablecloths protect and decorate at the same time. This casual fringed cloth is just right for a kitchen/dining room; choose printed cotton for a pretty look, damask or lace for a formal, traditional setting.

FACESAVERS

● Make a co-ordinating shower curtain by sewing a light cotton curtain to hang outside a plain white or pastel-coloured nylon one.

● Cover two squares of foam in fabric, add a scalloped, café curtain heading and hang them from a curtain pole to create a cheap and comfortable bedhead.

● Create a dressing table by covering a length of worktop with fabric topped by glass. Add ruffled skirts, a valance, and a stool with a matching seat – no-one will know the difference!

● Loop coloured ribbon through a lace tablecloth to pick up the colours of china or furnishings.

● Make a simple cover for a headboard, quilted for comfort if you like, and piped for a neat finish.

● Make a tie-on cover for a straight-backed dining chair that's past its best. Sew an envelope of fabric to slip over the back and a skirt with kick-pleats to just below the seat or to the floor and secure with matching ties.

● Cover an old, battered side table with a pretty, floor-length cloth and then drape a second, shorter one on top.

● Transform a pair of occasional tables by covering them – legs as well as top – in fabric to match or co-ordinate with curtains. Fix the top with photographers' display mount, mitre the corners and secure corners and seams with clear adhesive. Allow sufficient fabric for pattern matching and finish with clear varnish or top with bevelled-edge glass.

● Drape a table in floor-length plain sheeting by the yard and add swags of net, pinned in place with ribbon bows, for a celebration table.

● Staple two lengths of pleated cotton back-to-back to top and bottom battens (slats) and suspend them from the ceiling to form a screen or room divider.

CHAPTER 10

A sense of occasion

Furniture for decoration is one aspect of interior design that's often overlooked. Yet if you've put up the curtains, laid the carpet, added a border and *still* think that something's missing, it may be that you've concentrated on the shell of the room at the expense of its contents. Living is a 3-D affair and you need the right furniture to add substance and a variety of shapes and heights. A room which contains the bare essentials is likely to look empty, however much you decorate the walls, which is why you need a selection of decorative pieces to supplement the seating, dining table or bed.

It needn't cost a fortune. Some of the most interesting pieces can be bought second-hand for renovation, while cheap modern fibreboard can be transformed by simple paint treatments. If you are interested in collecting furniture, antique or modern, quality pieces are not only a pleasure to look at but have investment value also. It can be great fun looking for a bargain, too!

Right: Complementary shapes are as important to a scheme as colour and texture. Here curves predominate, on the round table and companion lamp and the wicker chair, offset by square cushions and linked by the soft colours and the floral theme.

Far right: Furniture as work of art – this classic Bauhaus lounger has a sculptural quality which makes it equally at home in an ultra-modern room or, as here, in a formal traditional setting.

SMALL TABLES

These are always useful. Indeed, it's difficult to do without a coffee table, which can be a problem in some traditional settings. If you're looking for antique or reproduction furniture consider a Pembroke or a sofa table. Pembrokes have drawers on each side and hinged flaps front and back which can be extended to form a low circular table. Sofa tables are a variation on the same theme with flaps on either side and drawers in front. Both are pretty – and pretty expensive. A butler's tray is another alternative or, for use on either side of a sofa, think about tables made from circles of plywood covered by pretty, layered cloths to co-ordinate with curtains – attractive yet inexpensive solutions.

Look at taller lamp tables which suit impressive table lamps, or abandon the search for symmetry and collect small gateleg, card or bamboo tables, stools and low chests. These are always worth acquiring if reasonably priced because they look attractive in so many rooms, whether supporting a jug of flowers in the hall or bathroom, used as bedside or occasional tables, or brought into use for informal suppers around the fireside or television.

Modern homes are easier to furnish because there are so many purpose-made designs. Choose between a large table in front of sofas (the most useful place, but it may get in the way), identical side tables, or a stacking set. Make sure that the design suits the style of its setting (don't mix black ash with pine unless you're sure that's the effect you want, for example) and paint cheap fibreboard tables or cover them with fabric (see page 83).

A modern console table in place of shelves or a storage unit is ideal if you only have a few items to display; they look equally impressive in halls, bedrooms and dining rooms. A glass-topped trestle table has a reflective quality that increases the impression of space and is large enough to double as a desk, dining or dressing table – though it will attract dust. The traditional equivalent is the writing or library table, but if you need more storage space think about a bureau or writing desk or a pretty Davenport (small desk) which has a sloping top and drawers down one side. Finally, look at glass and chrome or tubular steel trolleys (carts) to add interest in both shape and texture, suitable for a variety of modern interiors.

More dash than cash? Paint a wicker sofa, add a soft seat and a couple of cushions and you have a budget-price solution to the problem of furnishing the living room which will look equally effective in a bedroom or conservatory in years to come.

CHAIRS

These are cheap to buy and, whether new or second-hand, can be transformed by a coat of paint or a new seat cushion. Furnishing on a budget? Then consider radical alternatives to conventional furniture. A door or a length of plywood supported by trestles can be covered with sheeting to act as a floor-length tablecloth. Add the cheapest garden or folding chairs, stained and varnished in a colour which contrasts. Buy wicker furniture for the living room and fill with cushions – when you can afford the seating of your choice it can revert to its original role as garden or conservatory furniture.

Remember that you don't have to buy a dining table and chairs together. You can acquire the chairs first and the table later, or vice versa, as long as they look right together. Be careful, however,

about buying single dining chairs to make up a set, because there may be differences in the grain or colour which make two out of six look glaringly different. If you can get by with an odd number – five instead of six, for example – you may find some bargains in antique chairs, and it's always possible to add different carvers (chairs with arms, originally meant to be used at the head and foot of the table).

Styles worth collecting are nineteenth-century shield or balloon-back chairs, or old copies of the Regency Trafalgar chair with its curved sabre legs. You're unlikely to find a reasonably priced set but, bought singly, any of these make attractive bedroom chairs. Keep an eye out for tall, high-backed chairs (copies of eighteenth-century cane or turn-of-the-century Mackintosh designs, for example) to use in halls or where space is limited, but be careful when selecting a chair to team with a desk. If it's to be used for any length of time it must be comfortable and should support the small of the back. Working from home? Then it's hard to beat the special purpose-made typists' chair with its swivel seat which extends your reach.

When is a chair not a chair? When it's a chaise longue, or lounger. Don't think purely in terms of the traditional velvet-clad chaise longue, beautiful as it may be. There are many which add a sculptural quality to a modern setting, whether made from canvas, chromed steel and leather, or slatted wood like old-fashioned 'steamer' chairs.

Chairs can also be used as features in the living room, bedroom, bathroom and kitchen. Think about a traditional wing (wingback) chair or a chrome and leather chair to contrast with a pair of sofas; a button-back chair covered in a plain colour or a print which relates to the colour scheme; a basket chair in the bathroom; a Windsor chair in a country kitchen. Look for old, but newly fashionable, wicker-effect Lloyd Loom chairs sprayed to match your decor. Don't forget stools: you can stain classic beech and elm, choose brightly coloured steel tractor stools to suit a high-tech setting or use space-saving folding stools in black or red lacquer for an Oriental air.

STORAGE

This term covers cupboards and shelves, whether a grand breakfront bookcase, wall-to-wall fitments (units) in the living room or a row of kitchen units (cabinets). Shelves give you the opportunity of displaying as well as storing possessions. You could use one broad shelf-cum-worktop to accommodate the television, video and compact disc player, or fill alcoves each side of the fireplace with shelves for books. (Soften the look by mixing them with pictures and ornaments.) Remember that shelves like these must be strong and be supported every yard or metre if they are not to sag or collapse. Choose units with black offset shelves for an Oriental look, black, white or brightly coloured tubular steel for a high-tech one. Look out for small shelf units in second-hand shops or DIY (home improvement) stores. Strip, polish or stain the wood and fill with china, plants, collections or toiletries as the room demands. You'll need special shelves which keep plates upright if you want to display these, and you may feel happier with a guard rail to protect other types of china and glass.

Add glass doors and the shelves become a display cupboard. Many modern storage units are available with glass doors if this is the option you prefer, and they do deter both young children and dust. Traditional corner cupboards on the floor or wall bring interest to corners of the room, which are so often neglected, or use corner shelves filled with flowers and ornaments. Dressers and the more elaborate 'chiffoniers' combine cupboards and shelves in a useful and decorative storage unit which can replace conventional kitchen units (cabinets) or substitute for a sideboard in the dining room. The same effect can be achieved by placing a top unit (overhead cabinet) over a base cupboard or a chest of drawers. Many modular forms of wall-to-wall storage build up in this way, while smaller-scale designs use cubes, in natural wood or melamine (laminate) finish, either open or with shelves or doors.

IMPROVING FURNITURE

Don't reject unattractive or down-at-heel furniture out of hand – a little work will often transform a piece unrecognizably.

OLD FURNITURE

This may be scratched, dented or covered in hideous paint, but pieces more than 30 years old are probably made from solid wood and are often more decorative than modern styles. Before you buy, try to assess whether any clumsy repairs have been made and examine the piece for woodworm, which can be traced by the pattern of pinholes it leaves. (Always treat affected pieces with a special solution before you bring them indoors.) Next clean the article with diluted detergent to see what lies beneath the grime, taking care to wipe rather than

wash. Try rubbing pieces with a little methylated spirits to remove the finish (this works with french polish or shellac), otherwise sand it finely or use chemical stripper or a hot air gun to remove paint and varnish.

Now decide whether the piece is attractive as it is (in which case it can be polished or varnished) or whether it would look better with a fresh coat of paint to conceal imperfections. It may also need a few simple repairs. These may be cosmetic, like replacing missing mouldings (available from timber merchants – lumber yards in the US), disguising scratches by covering with crayon or packing with tinted wood filler, and cutting and filling burns.

The lines of this handsome cupboard were once hidden behind peeling paint. Stripped, sanded and varnished, it is now restored to its former beauty and makes an attractive and useful addition to this child's bedroom.

Here's a jokey design any-one can copy to liven up a cheap melamine (laminate)-finish chest of drawers. Prepare the base by applying two coats of eggshell paint (alkyd semigloss), sketch the design lightly on top with chalk or pencil before filling in, and finish with co-ordinating handles.

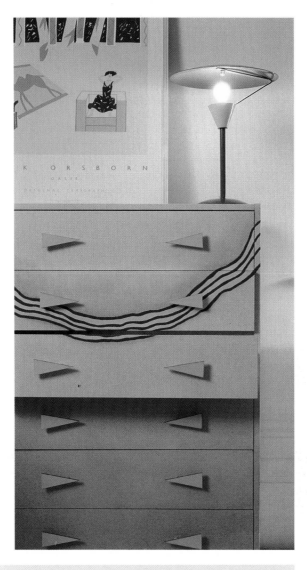

VARNISHING TECHNIQUES

Varnish is a transparent finish which won't conceal blemishes so careful preparation is required.

Bleach or stain the piece to a consistent colour. Filled patches and scratches should be coloured to match the surround, making them as inconspicuous as possible.

The next step is to sand the bare wood finely and give an initial coat of varnish diluted with 10 per cent white spirit. You'll achieve better results with a specially tapered varnish brush, but a new paint brush will do – don't use an old one or you will transfer traces of paint to the varnish.

Non-drip varnish is easier to control. Take care not to overload the brush (dip it into the tin or can so that half the bristle area is covered) and don't wipe the excess on the rim of the can as this may cause bubbles. Work evenly along the grain, maintaining a 'wet edge' because if the varnish is allowed to dry joins will show.

Work along shelf edges or uprights before brushing across from side to side and then finishing with one even stroke to eliminate brushmarks. You'll need to give at least one more coat, sanding lightly first to provide a key and wiping clean with white spirit. Allow the piece to dry in a still, dust-free atmosphere.

Dents can be raised by filling them or by pressing the area with a cloth wrung out in boiling water so that it swells.

More fundamental repairs include replacing chair stretchers (remember to drill out the old holes to remove the remains of the old stretcher and to clear away animal glue, which is incompatible with modern adhesives), replacing drawer runners or planing the edges to ensure that drawers don't stick. Joints may require new dowels, and hinges may need wall plugs to fill worn screw holes.

NEW FURNITURE

Modern furniture may be veneered (finished with fine layers of wood) or made from coated or plain particle board like chipboard which has no grain. Damaged veneer can be difficult to repair, especially if pieces are missing; it should be sanded as lightly as possible. It also blisters when wet; try ironing the area over a soft cloth and leaving a weight on top for a few days. Plain particle board is easier to treat, but remember to coat the absorbent edges with multi-purpose filler and sand finely before painting. Melamine (plastic laminate)-finished board can also be painted, provided it is sanded lightly first to provide a key. Take special care to avoid brush marks when applying paint, especially non-drip gloss.

Furniture made from particle board is usually simple in shape and benefits from being painted in bold colours, or with one of the techniques like sponging, stippling, combing or ragging. Don't forget stencils, which add a decorative flourish to plain chests, tables and toy boxes. If you're feeling adventurous you might like to try some of the advanced techniques such as vinegar graining (making patterns on coloured glaze with plasticine – modeling clay in the US) or fantasy marble or malachite finishes, made by manipulating paint and glaze to copy the effects of real stone.

SCREEN PLAY

Screens are moveable walls which can hide unsightly objects (a washbasin or clothes rail, for example) or act as room dividers. Traditional screens are made from three or four hinged panels, often covered with fabric or wallpaper. Modern 'see-through' versions include Oriental-style screens of black stained wood with paper panels, and screens made from steel mesh or natural wood lattice. Both types can be made at home. Create a see-through screen from louvres or trellis, or use

softwood panels covered with plywood (secured with glue and panel pins – nails in the US) for a solid screen. Cover with wallcovering or fabric, or paint the surface and stencil it to co-ordinate with existing furnishings.

GO FOR BURN

Although the fireplace is rarely the sole source of warmth in today's rooms, it makes a considerable contribution to the room's style. It's often worth re-opening a closed flue and replacing a fireplace for its decorative value alone. Try to find fireplaces which are in keeping with the age and style of your house, whether it's a Victorian villa or a thirties semi-detached house, and be careful before you rip

out original fittings which may become period pieces in time. It's still possible to buy salvaged Victorian cast iron grates and tiles but they are becoming increasingly scarce. Reproduction models of nineteenth-century fireplaces and stoves for Victorian and Edwardian houses and Adam-style mantelpieces in pine or white marble finish for Georgian and neo-Georgian homes are readily available. Fireplaces needn't look out of place in modern houses, either. Rooms can look very attractive with a slim 'Pither' stove or a variation on the hole in the wall fireplace.

Traditional fireplaces may be less efficient than modern ones and are more expensive to equip. The mantelpiece is usually separate and you may want a

A wired glass screen forms a transparent room divider which gives interest to this long room without absorbing the light. Its simple lines have been chosen to suit the formal furniture arrangement.

Every open fire needs a guard, and a full-size nursery guard is especially recommended if there are children in the house.

Remember that an attractive fireplace is the natural focal point of the room at all seasons. When it's not in use, fill the hearth with green plants or fresh or dried flowers – or choose good-quality artifical ones (not plastic). Silk arrangements look especially convincing. Alternatively, opt for an old-fashioned firescreen, either a reproduction or one which you've been lucky enough to pick up second hand and covered to match the decor.

OPENING A FLUE

Where there's a chimney there's a fireplace, even if it's hidden behind bricks – difficult to remove – or hardboard or plasterboard – relatively easy. Investigate by locating the chimney breast which will jut inside the room or outside the house. In a brick house it should have an air brick set into an inside wall for ventilation; remove this carefully. If there is no air brick, take away a few bricks about 12 inches (30 cm) above the floor. Light a candle to see whether the flame is drawn up the chimney, which indicates whether or not it is clear. Now unblock the opening, taking care not to disturb the lintel across the top of the fireplace which supports the upper brickwork. If the fireback is still in place, check that it is still usable, and seek expert advice on the size of fire and hearth you will require. (You may want to fit a 'throat' to restrict the draught, for example.) Finally, have the chimney thoroughly swept to clear away birds' nests and any other debris which may have collected there.

Fill a grate with flowers to make the most of a fireplace out of season and provide a focal point all year round. Choose green plants for a more lasting arrangement, silk or dried flowers for a permanent one.

fender to define the hearth. In addition, large fireplaces may need a separate fire basket, especially if you burn logs. You will also need to provide a coal scuttle or log basket and a brush and shovel or hearth set for cleaning and filling the grate, unless you opt for the warmth without work provided by one of the gas log fires on the market.

FACESAVERS
- Create a novelty screen to hide clutter in a child's room by painting a townscape or traffic scene in bold colours on to three panels of softwood-backed plywood.
- Use low chests in place of occasional tables; they provide storage too.
- Use cheap pleated paper roller blinds to serve as a screen.
- Install a deep shelf to double as a small dining table or desk. Paint it with brightly coloured gloss and add coloured steel or wooden chairs painted to match.
- Fit a worktop and shelves over cupboards and chests painted one colour for budget storage.

- Clean old bamboo with dilute soap flakes and borax and rinse with salt water. Wipe untreated cane with a solution of washing soda.
- 'Lose' unsightly cupboard doors by painting them to blend with the walls or covering the panels with matching wallpaper.
- Revive old-fashioned appliances by painting with brilliantly coloured smooth enamel (remember to use heat-resistant enamel on cookers and stoves).
- Save an old table by tiling the top to co-ordinate with the decor.
- Cut down a wobbly table to create a large coffee table or a slightly higher 'supper' table for informal meals.

PART THREE

AN EYE FOR DETAIL

Forget about family silver or portraits in oils because it's not what you have but how you display it which counts. Reject the mantelpiece syndrome which dictates that accessories are lined up in a row; instead display them where they contribute to the decor, putting plates on walls, lace in boxes or a collection of treasures in a frame. Remember that fixtures like door knobs and taps are important to the look of a room and above all, have fun acquiring the furniture, collecting the china and growing the plants which make your home unique.

Make an entrance

'OUT-DOORS'

First impressions count – and the first impression visitors receive of your home is given by your front door. It's essential that it suit your house and neighbourhood. If you live in an area where there is a mixture of house styles you can afford to indulge your own taste, but where houses are built to match, say in a Victorian terrace (series of row houses) or on a modern estate (tract development), think carefully about the effect it will have on the street before you replace the front door.

If the original door has long gone, choose one that's in keeping with the style of your home. A large Georgian house, for example, would normally have had an impressive panelled door complete with fanlight. A nineteenth-century terraced cottage (row house) would have had a far simpler panelled door (not a dinky version of a grander style), while rural cottages usually had solid, heavy doors to keep out the draughts which would otherwise have whistled straight through the front room. Thirties doors often featured decorative stained glass, while modern doors are often predominantly made of glass to allow light into the hall.

There are two main sources of doors: timber merchants (lumber yards) or DIY (home improvement) stores which sell new doors, and demolition contractors or architectural salvage firms which supply them second-hand. Many new doors have glass panes or an integral fanlight, though this is architecturally incorrect: the fanlight should be above, not part of, the door. A more accurate traditional style is the solid door with the classic four panel style. Whichever you choose, look for stout doors 2 inches (4.5 cm) thick or more for security and durability. Doors may be made from softwood (like fir) or hardwood (like mahogany). The cheaper softwoods are usually painted. If you want to use varnish you may need to pay more for an attractive hardwood grain and it's often necessary to stain the doors first. Second-hand doors are usually best painted as these are often blemished. Although it's convenient to buy an old door ready-stripped, stripping at home with a chemical or a hot air gun (not a blowtorch which may scorch the wood) is a better option as the caustic acid often used for commercial stripping may affect the glue and cause the joints to disintegrate.

Right: Mellow varnished wood is the ideal choice to offset this stained glass surround. Remember that the door must be in good condition as varnishing will reveal every flaw and that it's important to use exterior-grade varnish which will resist weathering.

Above left: This panelled front door with its graceful fanlight, twin pillars and marble step, found in the grander period homes, has been painted bright red to give a warm welcome.

Below left: Less formal but equally attractive, this front door is painted grey with the panels outlined in white for emphasis. The shrub in the pot is in keeping with the style and provides greenery all year round.

Above: Exotic painted panels make a feature of this conventional door. Extend the idea by painting all the doors in the hall on a common theme – substitute stencils for paintings unless you are sure of your skill.

Far right: This door is given interest by the mirror hung next to it, which echoes the shape and size of the door's glass panel. The mirror also reflects the door of the bedroom it faces and makes the most of limited light.

PAINT AND VARNISH

This must resist weathering, so make sure that the brand you choose is suitable for outside use. Remove all door furniture (hardware) before refinishing and use a solvent-based primer on new wood before painting. You may need two applications of undercoat with some types of exterior gloss and, if varnishing, you must apply at least three coats of a suitable type; restrict this to wood that's in good repair as it will not conceal flaws. There's a set order for finishing panelled doors which ensures good results. Start with the mouldings, then paint the panels, the central verticals, horizontals, sides, edges and frames, and remember to treat the bottom edge to protect the door from rot.

Front doors are often painted a bold colour for impact. Red, yellow, french navy and dark green are favourites, but black and white and neutrals like buff and grey can look equally smart. Some gloss colours are designed to blend with masonry paint to ensure a co-ordinated scheme. Remember that conservation (historic) areas and listed buildings may limit your choice of colour, so check before you begin work if your home is affected.

DOOR FURNITURE (HARDWARE)

The front door needs the works – door handles or knobs, a bell push, security lock, a number, letter box, bolts and possibly a door chain too – so it's important to co-ordinate this array of ironmongery. Choose door furniture (hardware) to complement the style of the door and the house. Heavy ironwork is best for cottages and mock-Tudor homes; delicate brass suits an eighteenth-century or neo-Georgian house, while sturdier shapes go with Victorian and Edwardian homes; simple chrome or stainless steel look effective on most post-Second World War housing. If you are in doubt about the style, always opt for a simple design rather than one that's too ornate. Is a lion's head knocker really right for your home, or would you feel happier facing the world with plain brass? Remember to provide an adequate letterbox, preferably at waist rather than ground level (or install a separate post box) and don't forget security. You should fit a mortice lock, with a night-latch (dead bolt) which can be locked from inside as well as out, and bolts, which prevent the door being forced off its hinges. You may also want a spyhole or security chain. Restrict access to the back of the house as French windows and patio doors, even with special locks and bolts, are always more vulnerable to burglars.

'IN-DOORS'

There's a wider choice of interior doors as these need not be weather- or burglar-proof. The three main types are the ledge and brace door (made from planks of wood), the panelled door and the flush door (made from a single sheet of board). All are available ready-made, though you may prefer to commission a door to fit an awkward opening.

Ledge and brace doors are traditional cottage doors. They are made from softwood, for painting or staining. The stronger type with diagonal cross-bars is suitable for outdoor use.

Panelled doors can be bought new or second-hand in traditional four- or six-panel designs or in variations on the period theme. The most expensive are made from solid hardwood such as mahogany or oak, but cheaper versions consist of softwood for painting, or a softwood or fibreboard core laminated with a hardwood facing, usually mahogany, designed to be stained and varnished.

Gleaming brass lion's head knocker and bell push are the perfect companions for this classic black Georgian front door. Keep brass door furniture in prime condition by regular polishing or buy types which have a protective lacquer finish.

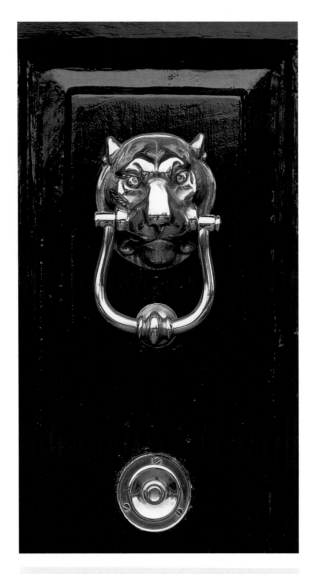

CARING FOR BRASS

Brass needs regular attention to preserve the finish and prevent corrosion. It may be plated ('bright' brass) or solid and is sometimes protected by a clear lacquer finish.

Lacquered brass should simply be wiped clean. If the finish is damaged, remove it with acetone (nail varnish remover) and polish with a proprietary (patented) cleaner before recoating.

Untreated brass should be washed with detergent solution to which a teaspoon of ammonia is added to remove grime. Dry with a soft cloth and then polish.

Corrosion can be treated with a lemon dipped in salt or a stiff paste made from equal amounts of vinegar, flour and salt. In severe cases try hydrochloric acid, but wear protective gloves and use tongs as the acid is highly corrosive.

Flush doors range from simple plywood to plywood, chipboard or hardboard faced with either a hardwood veneer or a white or simulated wood finish. It's also possible to buy 'embossed' doors with decorative mouldings to resemble panelled doors. If you feel that your home would originally have had panelled doors, investigate to see if these are hidden beneath flush panels which can be gently prised away.

PAINT AND VARNISH

These are not the only treatments for interior doors because here you have the option of polish too. Decide whether you want to make a feature of the door or whether it should blend with the decor. In a cluttered hall, for example, it's a good idea to 'lose' doors by painting them, along with the skirting (baseboard) and frame, to merge with the walls. On the other hand, if there are no architectural features and the doors are symmetrically placed, try painting them in a contrasting colour. Panelled doors in bedrooms can look pretty papered or sponged to match the walls, while white mouldings make a crisp contrast. Veneered flush doors may have a protective finish that only needs wiping down. If you want to change the colour of this type of door, test the treatment in an inconspicuous place to assess the type of finish, its depth, and its effect on colour.

DOOR FURNITURE (HARDWARE)

On interior doors the furniture can range from a simple black latch for cottage doors or a chrome, brass or china lever handle for flush doors to a full set of door knob, finger plate, and escutcheon or key plate for panelled doors. These 'suites' are available in plain or decorated brass or brass plate, and plain white or decorated china; stripes, flowers and fruit are equally popular. If you just want a simple door knob, there are wood, plastic and cut glass too. Make sure that all the door furniture (hardware) in a room relates, linking cupboard and drawer knobs and handles to the style of those used at the entrance. It's not essential to buy a matching set; you can add to the individuality of your house by collecting old door knobs and finger plates, but remember that the style should suit the formality of the door or furniture to which it is attached. A set of elaborate cabinet handles may be just what's needed to finish a mahogany chest of drawers, for example, but stripped pine looks better with plain china and laminate kitchen units (cabinets) call for contrasting coloured plastic.

Put the cat out every night with this trompe l'oeil detail which enlivens a simple front door. The white recess, dark surround and scarlet door make a bright spot out of what was once a dingy passageway.

FACESAVERS

• Stipple or marbleize the interior of your front door to give impact inside as well as out.

• Pressed flowers behind plain glass finger plates give a charming old-fashioned air.

• Paint white china door knobs and finger plates with enamel. Stencil a trellis pattern or stipple or flick a design to co-ordinate with your colour scheme.

• Pick out the mouldings on a panelled door in a contrasting colour to emphasize the effect of walls or soft furnishings.

• Use two half-width doors in place of one where space is limited.

• Upgrade kitchen units (cabinets) by fitting plain brass or white china door knobs in place of the handles provided.

• Add interest to flush doors by painting a stripe or stencilling a border along the skirting (baseboard) and around the architrave – flank it with neo-classical plywood pillars and add an arch overhead for a really over-the-top effect!

• Paint flush doors in contrasting primary colours against white, grey or pale yellow walls for a modern art effect.

• Make flush doors more formal by adding wooden beading to create false panels.

• Fit louvre doors to wardrobes (built-in closets) against outside walls to prevent damp, and to the airing cupboard to allow heat to circulate.

CHAPTER 12

Taps and tiles

Kitchens and bathrooms always look smart when they feature these perfect partners. Tiles provide instant style and practicality, forming a hardwearing barrier to the damage that water can do to the fabric of our homes.

TILE STYLE

It's hard to beat tiles for durability and elegance. What other finish is waterproof, lasts for years and needs no more care than regular sweeping and mopping? That's true not only of ceramic and quarry tiles but of vinyl and vinyl-coated cork too. Use them for floors, especially in small or awkwardly shaped rooms, for walls, as splashbacks or decorative panels, and as a cover for shelves, tables and worktops. Remember to limit their use in cool climates, where they can look cold, and to choose colours and patterns which contribute to the colour scheme.

CERAMIC TILES

Made from glazed pottery, ceramic tiles come in a wide range of designs. Highly glazed, boldly coloured and patterned tiles are designed for walls, while floors need a more robust, slightly textured tile. Wall tiles are usually 4½ inches (108 mm) or 6 inches (152 mm) square, and floor tiles 8 inches (200 mm) square, although rectangular, hexagonal and Provençal shapes are also available. You'll find a greater variety of designs in wall tiles than those for the floor because practical considerations like safety, resistance to wear and dirt need to be taken into account for the latter. Few wall tiles are durable enough for floors. They may withstand wear in a bathroom or shower room but only a few will be suitable for a hall or conservatory so check before you buy.

Bathroom, kitchen or even fireplace tiles can be the focal point of your scheme but don't let them clash with other colours and designs. If you already have heavily patterned curtains or wallpaper, opt for self-coloured, geometric or sculpted tiles rather than pictorial designs. If the surroundings are plain you can choose Victorian reproductions, screen-printed abstract designs, hand-painted florals or a mural built up from individual tiles. Some designs are formed by four or more tiles and there are some charming jokey notions – like cat and bird sequences, for example. Just make sure that the joke won't wear thin and become irritating after a time!

Remember that patterned tiles don't have to be used en masse. Consider creating a square or a border by using a row of patterned tiles in an area of white or making a panel of patterned tiles sur-

Right: Ceramic tiles have a classic elegance, creating a floor that's hard-wearing and easy to clean. Plain tiles, like those shown here, make the most of space, while patterned tiles often become the focal point of the room.

Far right: Red and white vinyl tiles add impact to this modern kitchen. The squares repeat the pattern and colour of the wall-mounted grid and the design of the blind and window-pane check wallpaper.

rounded by plain. Collect antique tiles to set on a window ledge or to display on plate hangers; you can incorporate them into a row of modern tiles, too, provided the thickness is compatible.

Don't forget worktops (counters). Ceramic tiles make a hard-wearing, washable surface which will resist heat from pans and some designs have special edge tiles and corner pieces for a curved finish. A tiled worktop is heavy, so don't tile over an existing surface unless you're sure that it can take the

strain. You'll need to use epoxy grout to ensure hygiene, but even so dirt will collect between the tiles – use a toothbrush dipped in bleach to clean the grout from time to time.

Think about border tiles to provide a neat finish for splashbacks. A contrasting edging strip can give an expensive air to plain tiles and it's also possible to buy banded tiles, with a brightly coloured top stripe. Alternatively, finish off with beading.

Ceramic tiles on walls and floors are by far the

In a small bathroom, use identical tiles on the floor, as a splashback, and on the bath panel to create an impression of space. Choose a pale colour and a plain finish with a border or corner design, as here, for interest.

easiest type to clean. All they need is a regular mopping with warm water and washing up liquid, then a rinse and a rub with a dry cloth to shine.

QUARRY TILES

These unglazed ceramic tiles are traditionally used for hall and kitchen floors and are also suitable for worktops. They look splendid in cottage kitchens and are durable and easy to care for, *provided* that you accept that the finish is supposed to be matt. If you apply tile paint or strive for a shine you are creating unnecessary work and possibly spoiling the effect of the tiles. Most quarries are deep red, though black, buff and brown are also available.

They are thicker than most ceramic tiles, are usually laid in a bed of mortar and can be difficult for the layman or woman to cut, so professional installation is recommended.

CORK TILES

Cork is warm and resilient but because it is absorbent, the tiles need careful sealing in 'wet' areas like the bathroom or kitchen. You should either coat them with at least three layers of polyurethane varnish or buy ready-treated tiles. Special sealed cork tiles are available now, which have been dipped in vinyl to seal even their edges to provide greater resistance to moisture, but you must expect to pay

Floor-to-ceiling ceramic tiles provide an elegant and practical wallcovering in classic blue and white for this large kitchen. Panels of plainer border pattern tiles are used to define work stations and increase visual space.

considerably more for this type than for ordinary sealed cork tiles. In other rooms cork tiles can be wax-polished, but remember that this entails regular maintenance. Most cork tiles are large – 12 inches (300 mm) square – and a pleasant neutral brown which blends with many schemes, but choose tiles with coloured veins (red, green and black are popular) or plain white if you want the floor to co-ordinate with your decor.

Untreated cork can be used on walls to create a pinboard. Slot tiles between shelves or cupboards, finish with wooden beading or surround the cork with a stencilled border to create a frame. Thick dark insulating cork adds warmth but should be used with care as it can look oppressive. It is effective used to ceiling height in place of a headboard in a teenager's room, to form a panel above a desk, or to make a wide frieze in a playroom, covered with a display of junior works of art offset by bright primary colours.

VINYL TILES

These are often inexpensive and may be self-adhesive for do-it-yourself use, though solid vinyl for professional installation – which rivals ceramic tiles in price – is available.

Tiles, which are usually 12 inches (300 mm) square, are more versatile than sheet flooring because you can use them to create your own designs. Why not make a border of plain coloured tiles to contrast with a floor that's mainly cream or grey, for example? Alternatively, mix tiles in blocks of colour – red, white, blue and yellow – for an abstract art effect. (Look at a painting by Mondrian for inspiration.) Design a 'pathway' along a hall or across a dining room or kitchen, or make a panel by using patterned tiles in the centre of a plain floor. Remember that contrasting skirting (baseboards) will add life to the plainest flooring and brighten up plainly furnished rooms such as kitchens and halls. If you prefer a more formal look, lay flecked black and white tiles in diamonds for a fake marble effect or, for a variation on the theme, buy white tiles with pastel or primary coloured corners.

Vinyl tiles are extremely practical and too useful to relegate to kitchens and bathrooms; use them for a stylish and easy-care flooring in playrooms, dining rooms and halls as well.

Vinyl tiles should never be cleaned with an abrasive powder, as this may scratch their surface. Textured types should not be allowed to get too grimy, as they can be difficult to clean.

Above: White tiles have a reflective quality which makes them ideal for use in rooms with limited light. The geometric border design adds interest and relates to the bold blue which surrounds the windows.

Left: Contrast grouting looks chic and gives plain white tiles a fashionable grid effect. Increase the impact in a bathroom by using tiles on the floor as well as on the walls and add cool white bathroom ware to match.

TYPES OF TILE

Universal tiles (the majority) are glazed on two or four edges and are chamfered for use anywhere in the tiled area.

Field or spacer tiles are glazed only on the face for use in the centre of a tiled area.

Edge or border tiles have a curved edge on the top or on two sides, for use at corners and edges.

Mosaic tiles come on a backing sheet. They are particularly useful for tiling areas full of obstacles such as pipes, as individual tiny squares can be peeled off.

In addition, some tiles have lugs which act as built-in spacers when grouting; others need separate plastic spacers; and universal tiles have bevelled edges which butt against each other, leaving a gap for the grout.

Far right: A monobloc mixer tap (faucet) in chrome sets a shining example in this modern kitchen, teamed with a fine Venetian blind (miniblind), tall fitted cupboards (cabinets), plain creamy walls and an inset sink in stainless steel.

TAPS (FAUCETS)

There's more to a tap (faucet) than a chrome pillar and an acrylic-covered head! Taps should complement the style of your sink or bathroom ware and there's now a wide range of reproduction designs to suit Victorian and Edwardian china sinks, bath-tubs and washstands, as well as sleek or brightly coloured modern designs.

TAP HEADS

Technical improvements include ceramic discs which do not wear and which are gradually replacing old-fashioned rubber washers, and anti-splash features to ensure a smooth flow. The tapheads define the style. Most modern designs are 'shrouded' in clear acrylic, though plain or coloured metal, onyx, marble and decorated ceramic heads are available. You'll also find lever controls on mixer taps, which can be turned on with a flick of the wrist, especially useful in the kitchen where your hands may be full. Traditional taps in chrome or brass have crossheads, though you will also be able to find Edwardian-style lever taps if you prefer. Pastels and bright colours are sometimes used to give this shape modern appeal.

PILLAR TAPS

This term is used to describe individual taps which separate hot water from cold. In the UK kitchen taps are usually higher than bathroom pillars so that pans can be held beneath. These are seldom found in the US anymore.

MIXER TAPS

This type has a spout which mixes hot with cold. Kitchen mixers should have two channels inside the spout so that the cold drinking water is kept entirely separate from the stored hot water. There are several different styles.

Monobloc mixers combine mixer spout and hot and cold taps in one fitting. These may be a rotating ball or cartridge type.

Deck mixers have a bridge for the spout between the two taps, which require separate holes.

Three hole mixers need separate connections for each tap and the spout.

Bath mixers have a shower attachment to which water is diverted by means of a simple lever. And you will find that it's also possible to buy a thermostatically controlled bath mixer to regulate the water temperature.

Below: Problem – which tap (faucet) should you use for a traditional kitchen? Answer – try period-style cross-head mixer taps like this attractive brass design for upstairs/downstairs use.

FACESAVERS

• Make the most of expensive hand-painted ceramic tiles by using them as accents on steps or window sills.

• Use a collection of old, decorative tiles to create a *trompe l'oeil* rug to brighten up the centre of an otherwise plain tiled floor.

• Use contrasting coloured grouting with plain tiles to create a high-tech grid effect.

• Use ceramic mosaic tiles on sheets which split into individual pieces when tiling awkward areas.

• Lay frostproof tiles to create a traditional patterned doorstep.

• Use broken tiles to create a colourful mosaic, either abstract or in a shape like a fish in a kitchen, shells in a bathroom. Keep the design simple for successful results.

• Add interest to a boring splashback by using a wallpaper border above the tiles in a relating colour and design.

• For an integrated look and as a visual space-stretcher, tile the bath surround with ceramics, cork or vinyl to match the floor.

CHAPTER 13

Pictures and mirrors

Pictures, photographs, books and pieces of china make a room personal. The most immaculately decorated room looks soulless without them, which is why stylists who create settings for advertisements and magazines spend hours in antique shops and flea markets searching for paintings and accessories which make a room look more of a home and less of a set.

While most of us know what we like in the way of books and china, we're less certain when it comes to art. Choosing a painting is a declaration of taste that's made for all to see – hence the popularity of neutral subjects like landscapes and reproductions of acknowledged works of art. Few of us buy pictures in sufficient numbers to acquire confidence in our judgment, or to create an attractive display. Many people make the mistake of choosing one or two large pictures and hanging them on adjacent walls, which minimizes their impact. Considering paintings simply as an extension of the colour scheme, chosen to 'go with' paint or soft furnishings, is another common error. Would you turn down a Picasso because it was blue? The truth is that most paintings can be hung in most settings provided sufficient attention is paid to position, frame and mount.

And while you're considering how to enhance your walls, don't neglect the potential of mirrors. As well as being effective space-stretchers they may provide a decorative element in themselves.

COLLECTING PICTURES

What is a picture? It can be an original painting, a print, a sketch, a reproduction (essentially a photograph of a painting), an actual photograph, a magazine cover, or a plate from a book. It can also be three-dimensional; you can frame a collage, a collection (of button hooks or shells, for example), a piece of lace or pressed flowers. These 'homemade' pictures are invaluable for showing your interests and for padding out a collection of paintings that's still in its infancy. Look in antique shops and sales for old paintings, prints, silhouettes and samplers. There won't be many bargains, but you may find attractive pictures at a reasonable cost.

Original paintings are expensive, though visits to local galleries and end-of-term displays at art colleges can yield paintings that are both interesting

and modestly priced – and you may have the thrill of seeing your chosen artist's work become more widely known (and more valuable). Be guided by instinct if you're aware that your knowledge is limited. If you feel there is something wrong with the perspective, the use of light and shade, or the way an arm is drawn – you're probably right. Don't buy paintings you won't feel at home with unless you're collecting purely for investment, but do approach pictures with an open mind. This is one case where impulse buys are often the best. If a painting appeals and it won't break the bank, buy it. If you go away to think it over, you're bound to find another way of spending money, and a meal out can never equal the lasting pleasure a painting will give. Remember that you will get what you pay for and if you commission a portrait for a small amount of money it will be a quick sketch, not an oil-painting!

When buying a print, there are certain questions to ask so that you can be sure you know what you are getting. How 'limited' is a limited edition? Is the print an etching, made by using acid on a metal plate, or a woodcut, printed from an engraving on wood? Is the picture an original print, where the artist has made the block, or a photographed reproduction? Find out whether antique prints have been hand-coloured or otherwise retouched and whether those charming illustrations are copies or originals.

FRAMING

Frames should complement both the painting and the style of your room. Choose ornate gilt mouldings for a traditional portrait or landscape in a period or neo-classical room, a simple steel or black frame for a boldly coloured abstract in a modern setting. Special pictures are best professionally framed unless you have the skill and equipment to cut glass and mitre mouldings at home; ask to see the full range of mouldings and mounts the shop or gallery can supply. Don't choose too thin a moulding or the frame will not have sufficient strength: the width of the moulding should measure at least one-twentieth of the picture's longest side.

Traditional frames may be made from hardwood (such as walnut), and gilt, black lacquer and gilt, mock tortoiseshell, 'antiqued' gilt, carved wood or gilt-covered plaster with elaborate details like acorns and leaves.

This constant height picture arrangement on a common theme forms a panel which emphasizes the symmetry of this room, with its matching chairs placed each side of the occasional table.

This arrangement takes as its central point the ornate mantel clock on the chest beneath. Pictures are displayed on each side, allowing plenty of room to extend the arrangement as new paintings are acquired.

Because large, elaborate frames are so expensive, it's often a good idea to rescue old frames. Be prepared to commission or carry out a number of repairs, because mitred corners often come apart, the mouldings may need stripping and staining and plaster work may need patching and gilding.

Modern frames are usually simpler, though you will find lined, stained, stippled and lacquered wood mouldings, as well as ready-made steel and plastic frames.

Mounts (mattes) are important because they make the picture stand out from its surround, which is vital if you have patterned walls. Although their use is normally optional, it's essential to use mounts (mattes) when framing watercolours so that condensation beneath the glass does not make the paint run. Take time to choose the mount (matte) as it should enhance the picture, the frame, and the wall behind. You will also want to choose colours which relate if you are hanging pictures in a group. Traditional scenes usually need softer colours than modern paintings; be guided by the overall impression given by the picture. Is it a lively sailing scene in sharp blue and white with splashes of red? Then you can afford to pick a livelier colour for the mount

(matte) than for a sombre seascape in grey, green and indigo. Choose soft colours for gentle paintings and bright for bold. You have a choice of texture too, and here it's best to err on the side of simplicity: a silk or linen finish is attractive but the mount (matte) shouldn't compete with the painting.

The size of the mount (matte) should be one-tenth of the longest side of the picture. Modern mounts (mattes) are often constant in size, but traditional picture framers use what is called the 'golden ratio', with extra depth at the base to give more pleasing proportions. The golden ratio is a complex mathematical formula, but a rule of thumb is to allow 25 per cent extra at the base of the picture, or more if you want the title and name of the artist inset.

Glass is not essential for varnished oil paintings or for block-mounted posters, which are protected by a layer of film. Large pictures need 1/8 inch (3 mm) thick glass while tiny ones are best with thinner than 1/16 inch (2 mm), though this is often difficult to obtain. Non-reflective glass is a wise choice if pictures are near or opposite windows, but try not to hang original paintings where they may be affected by sunlight as the colours may fade.

Ready-made frames are for the times when you don't want to go to the expense of having a frame purpose-made. Perhaps you want to hang enlarged snapshots and children's paintings or certificates, or decorate the kitchen with illustrations from a cookery book or magazine. You may be fond of a certain greetings card or poster, but not be prepared to spend far more than the picture is worth on the frame. The answer is to buy from the wide range of ready-made frames, available in white or coloured plastic, aluminium, stained or bleached wood, or mosaic finish, or as a frameless frame where pictures are sandwiched between glass and backing board and held in place by stainless steel clips. Ready-made frames are not as robust or as showy as purpose-made frames, and frameless frames will not protect the picture from dust or damp, but the advantage is that it's easy to change the contents when you tire of them.

HANGING PICTURES

Try to 'anchor' the position of paintings to that of furniture or architectural details. A painting that's isolated in the middle of a wall contributes little to the room and won't attract the attention it deserves. Reserve this treatment for very large pictures or posters which are imposing enough on their own and which would dwarf paintings hung nearby.

Don't hang pictures too far above eye level, where they cannot be appreciated, or too low, where they may be knocked off-centre. The best way to arrange them is to lay all the pictures you possess on the floor and experiment with different groups. It's wise to have the largest picture no bigger than one-third the size of the total group, but you can mix oval and hexagonal shapes with conventional rectangular frames to add interest. To ensure an effective arrangement, aim for constant height or depth or for constant spacing.

Constant height or depth is easiest because it simply involves aligning the base or top of the pictures. This form of grouping works particularly well above low sofas, tables or chests, but it's important to bring the group close to the level of the furniture as large expanses of wall between the two will spoil the effect. There's no need to complete the group straightaway. If you align the left-hand sides of the pictures as well as the base or top, the group will look composed and you will have sufficient space to add more paintings later.

Constant spacing produces an irregular shape, but harmony is maintained because all the paintings are the same distance apart – a maximum of 4 inches (100 mm), depending on their size. Here it's best to start with a central group of three or four pictures and to extend the display upwards and outwards as your collection grows. This is also a good way of arranging pictures in a stairwell. Think about a triangular shape which has its apex towards the top of the flight of stairs, but try to avoid a mannered 'stepped' arrangement.

Sometimes it's possible to have a completely constant arrangement of pictures where all are the same size – a collection of flower prints or street scenes, for example. Where pictures vary greatly in size, consider separate groupings, so that the small ones are not overwhelmed, and hang the smaller pictures where they are most prominent so that they will not be overlooked. 'Theme' arrangements often work well; choose herbs for the kitchen, flowers or dancers for the bedroom, and ships for the bathroom.

Picture rails are designed to take the weight of heavy pictures, preferably suspended by two lengths of picture cord, picture wire, or (for very heavy paintings) chain. Using the picture rail for the purpose for which it's designed is not compulsory, and you may prefer to use wall-mounted picture hangers if you dislike the look of traditional picture cord on your walls.

Four flower pictures in identical frames form a bold panel and give a brilliant splash of colour to the plain walls. Use pieces of fabric, wrapping paper or wallcovering to create a similar effect at next-to-no cost.

Prettier than plain picture cord, bows hold these prints in place. The arrangement looks striking set against the red and white gingham ground.

ON REFLECTION

Mirrors have an almost magical effect on light and space. They are invaluable in small rooms, which they can seem to double in size, and in dark ones, where they reflect the light. They can be used architecturally, as wall-to-ceiling panels where you are conscious only of the effect, or decoratively, where intricate or brightly coloured frames and bold shapes are as important as the mirror itself.

POSITION

For architectural use, the edges of the mirror should be concealed in an alcove or by mouldings. Experiment before you affix the mirror in place so that you are satisfied with what it reflects. Don't place mirrors directly opposite seating so that the occupants are constantly confronted by an image of themselves, at the top of the stairs or the end of the hall (where meeting yourself can be unnerving), or immediately opposite a door, where the double image may look confusing. Try to reflect plants, ornaments and attractive features, and consider using mirror as a splashback or fitting it behind shelves to increase the impact of their contents. You can increase light, too, by placing mirror next to or at right angles to a window. In a bedroom, mirror-clad wardrobes (closets) will also make the most of light and give you an all-round view of yourself; these are best suited to modern settings. Remember to make sure that the structure can take the weight if you add mirror to existing doors.

Decorative mirrors are traditionally used on walls (pier glasses) or over the fireplace (overmantel mirrors). Overmantel mirrors may have heavy, elaborate frames which look equally impressive in a hall or traditional bathroom, while pier glasses are

usually more delicate and oblong in shape. They were originally used between deep sash windows, still a good place for reflecting light, or behind narrow tables. Don't forget free-standing dressing table and cheval mirrors; these are particularly suited to period homes (though modern versions are also available). Etched and painted mirrors use their reflective quality to emphasize the design. These vary in quality, so choose with care – unless you are making a collection of 'pub art'. It is always possible to add ornament without relying on colour, decoration or the frame, by choosing an interesting shape, such as an oval, arch or wedge.

Left: Three items are used to decorate this hallway – the mirror, which increases the impact of the stained glass window, the china dog and the single small painting set alone on the far wall, the exception to the rule that pictures look best in groups.

FACESAVERS

● Single pictures can be hung above a shelf, small table or mantelpiece, or propped against the wall to form a composition with, say, a vase of flowers, a clock, or china. Don't automatically place the picture in the centre of the arrangement; it's often better hung asymmetrically to balance a tall object, like a lamp or vase, at the other end.

● Pictures have a place in every room. Use colour plates from recipe books or scene-setting pictures from magazine cookery pages in simple ready-made frames to decorate the kitchen.

Sandwich children's art between glass and backing board to hang in their bedrooms and choose cheap prints in pretty frames or block-mounted pictures to decorate the bathroom. (Don't put original paintings here or use frameless frames because steam may damage the pictures.)

● Give black and white prints importance by placing them in clip frames and surrounding each with a traditional black and white border to simulate an eighteenth-century print room.

● Display pictures against a plain or self-patterned (perhaps sponged or dragged) wall for best effect.

Far left: Use furniture, like the low sofa shown here, to define the limits of a picture arrangement. This collection can be both constant height and constant-spaced because the elements involved are identical in size.

CHAPTER 14

Pleasures of the table

Table settings create a sense of occasion, whether the meal is a family lunch or a formal dinner party – and they needn't involve effort or expense. A bunch of wild flowers in a pottery jug, crisp napkins and robust tumblers filled with *vin ordinaire*, fresh rolls laid out in a basket, a bowl of green salad and a plate of cheeses is better than a feast that's presented without adequate care. And when you do want to make an impression, there's nothing to match a formal place setting with silver cutlery, gold-rimmed china, crystal glassware, white damask cloth and napkins and tall candles to set the scene.

Whatever the style, take care to co-ordinate your table settings. Use sleek stainless steel cutlery with simple modern flatware and reserve elaborate silver plate for your bone china. Team heavy ironstone plates and beakers with wicker baskets on a scrubbed pine table; lay graphic design earthenware on a bright spotted cloth; use primary coloured plastic on laminate or PVC (vinyl). China in delicate shapes and soft colours needs fine-stemmed glassware and a lace or light cotton tablecloth, while formal bone china with gold, silver or cobalt trim looks best on traditional white linen. You'll probably find that you have two types of china – one for informal meals and another for special occasions. Make sure all your everyday china relates (it doesn't have to match) to make the most of every meal and put your best set on display for a visual feast.

CHINA

Bone china combines delicacy with strength, which may surprise those who treat it with reverence and save it for best. The secret lies in its composition, developed in the eighteenth century, which consists of 25 per cent kaolin (china clay), 25 per cent stone and 50 per cent bone ash to add whiteness and translucency.

Earthenware is made from common or 'ball' clay, flint and stone. It is used for everyday pottery and tableware and is also available in lovely traditional designs. Earthenware can be treated so that it can be used as ovenware, but it is less robust than fine or bone china as it chips easily and, when chipped, will absorb stains. As the fashion designs produced in earthenware often have a limited production run, it's worth buying extra plates and cups so that you

have a personal stock in case of breakages.

Fine china or English translucent china can be imagined as bone china without the bone; though strong and delicate, it lacks the translucent quality which is unique to bone china.

Porcelain preceded bone china and is quite different in construction, being made from 50 per cent kaolin plus 25 per cent quartz and 25 per cent felspar. It is strong, varies in thickness and can be used for oven to tableware.

Stoneware is made from a naturally vitrifying rock which means that the particles fuse as they do in glass. It is strong but thick and is used for ovenware as often as for pottery.

COLOUR

You can never have too much white china! White (with perhaps a fine gold, silver or cobalt rim) is the traditional choice for royalty, ambassadors, and the like, who frown upon patterned plates as not quite the thing. Even if you're not of that opinion, remember that white china is invaluable for supplementing patterned plates, and matching or replacing pieces is never a problem. White china can be very cheap, or very expensive; for versatility, choose fine china, earthenware, or even milky white glassware. Modern versions of the 'fine line' theme are available for those who want a touch of colour (ideal for mix-and-match designs). Fluted designs look pretty and complement fluted patterned china, and hexagonal shapes will make the most of an Art Deco collection. Plain colours, usually on earthenware, include the traditional Adam blue and calyx green, often used on designs taken from eighteenth-century silver, and modern designs in grey, bright primaries and contemporary pastels.

PATTERN

Pattern can be confined to a border or cover the surface. There is a wealth of traditional patterns on bone china and earthenware, like eighteenth-century tree of life and willow pattern designs, bird and flower patterns and pastoral scenes. Modern designs may be delicate, featuring flowers or fruit on fine china, or bold, with graphic designs on earthenware or rustic patterns on heavy pottery. Most patterns are made by painting or printing under the glaze, which provides a clear, impervious surface,

A meal becomes a special occasion when the table is laid with fine china and a pretty cloth. Gilt-edged white bone china is a classic choice, as suitable for a grand dinner as for morning coffee or afternoon tea.

CUTLERY

Silver-plated cutlery should be made to standards which ensure that the plate is thick enough to resist wear. Most designs are traditional and are often elaborate, but if you want a simple style look at classics like Georgian rat-tail or Old English patterns. Handles are often integral but may be made from bone or wood which may require more care and are often unsuitable for dishwashing. Second-hand canteens (sets) or bundles of cutlery are generally cheap and readily available but you will have more difficulty in acquiring knives because the handles may not last as long as the rest of the cutlery.

Stainless steel cutlery should also be made to a standard which guarantees the materials used and the strength of individual items. Inferior cutlery is liable to break or bend and should be avoided. Stainless steel cutlery is available in modern as well as traditional styles and is easy to care for. Though cutlery with separate handles, in wood, coloured plastic, or china, tends to be less robust than one-piece designs, you may be prepared to give them extra care in return for the contribution they make to your colour scheme.

HOW MUCH DO YOU NEED?

China is sold as individual items and as tea or coffee sets or dinner services, and it's usually possible to build up a collection of bone or fine china or traditional earthenware piece by piece. Most dinner services are composed of dinner, dessert and side plates, soup plates (or bowls or cups), fruit or cereal bowls, covered and open vegetable dishes, oval serving dishes (platters), and gravy boats. Coffee sets contain a coffee pot, cream jug (creamer), open or covered sugar bowl, plus cups and saucers. (Remember you'll need demi-tasse cups for after-dinner coffee.) Tea sets are made up of a teapot, milk jug (pitcher), sugar bowl, cups and saucers and often side plates and a bread and butter plate as well.

The advantage of buying single items is that you can select what you need. You may prefer one jug (pitcher) and sugar bowl for both tea and coffee, and you may not want a coffee pot if you have a separate coffee maker. For everyday use, you may restrict the list to dinner plates, side plates, and soup/cereal bowls, adding separate mugs, casseroles, serving dishes, jugs (pitchers) and teapot. You will need some china not included in the standard dinner service – oven-to-tableware, casseroles, soufflé and

How can you be formal when eating asparagus – or artichokes? Special dishes make it less of an ordeal, and this table setting strikes a comfortable balance, partnering fine china and silver cutlery with colourful tablemats and plain glasses.

but sometimes the pattern is formed by the shape, a trend dating back to last century. You'll find cabbage leaf plates and 'celery' jugs, as well as novelty apple, lemon and strawberry shapes which may appeal to you, and a number of decorative pieces with moulded designs. The glaze may be clear or coloured, for a translucent look, and may create a pattern itself; 'crackled' glaze pieces have an attractive crazed appearance.

GLASS

Glass may be either crystal or soda glass.

Crystal contains lead oxide, which gives it its characteristic brilliance and chime. The traditional facets of cut crystal are designed to reflect the light, but plain crystal is also available. Full lead crystal, the most expensive form, contains 30 per cent lead oxide and is usually hand-cut. Lead crystal contains 24 per cent and is not as costly; it may be machine-made.

Soda glass is made from sand, soda ash and limestone and is used for a range of very diverse items, from fine hand-blown goblets to moulded glass and mundane milk bottles.

gratin dishes, ramekins and a large milk jug, for instance. You may also want some special pieces, like a cake stand, a cheese plate, fruit and salad bowls, a fish platter, soup tureen or strawberry dish, but this depends on your individual needs.

Glass for everyday use should include robust tumblers and Paris goblets. For a dinner or lunch party you'll need large goblets for red wine, small for white, flutes for champagne, plus sherry, liqueur and brandy glasses. (Avoid very large wine glasses as most people count their consumption by the glass.) Use tumblers for spirits or fruit juice, and tall straight glasses for beer and mineral water. Complete the collection with water jugs and decanters.

Cutlery is reduced in most families to a minimum of knife, fork, butter knife, dessert fork and spoon and teaspoon each, plus a carving knife and fork and serving spoons. However, you may need extras for fish, plus soup spoons and special equipment like cheese and fruit knives, jam and egg spoons, lobster picks and salad servers which will all be useful when you are entertaining.

SETTINGS FOR SPECIAL OCCASIONS

When you're preparing food for a special occasion don't forget that the table, too, needs a little extra care. Try to match the tenor of the setting to the event, whether it is a formal christening or a noisy children's party.

PARTIES

Whether you're throwing a party for your friends or your children's friends, special table preparations always help the party spirit along.

Children's parties need a table setting with a theme. The table's appearance is often far more important than the food, for few young children eat more than sausages on sticks or hotdogs and an astonishing amount of crisps (potato chips). Three is the youngest age advisable, both for a successful 'unaccompanied' party and for one at which the guests may be persuaded to sit down. As the cake is usually the centrepiece, plan the table setting on a similar theme. If the cake is a train, for example, consider running a clockwork (wind-up)railway set round the table and provide jam tarts coloured like signals and brightly coloured fizzy drinks. A simple cake can be jazzed up with a colourful ribbon, with small toys or characters made from moulding icing on top. Consider an Alice in Wonderland party for an older girl, with Alice-like paper dolls as place markers, top hats made of paper and give-away Alice hairbands. Make 'goody' bags for the guests to take home, from colourful fabric tied with ribbon to form small bundles and use colourful paper or plastic tableware, cloth and napkins.

For older children, choose a colour theme and extend it to the food. A pink disco will be appreciated by most growing girls, but for mixed parties choose something sophisticated like black and white.

Adult parties are often buffets so as to cope with greater numbers. Hire (rent) trestle tables if necessary, cover them with white or coloured sheeting and buy remnants of co-ordinating patterned fabric to make napkins. Decide on a colour – green and white for a simple summer party where the staples are cheese, salad, fruit and crisp white wine; crimson and gold for a curry special, using brass trays and candlesticks and draping the table with appropriate ethnic prints. Arrange food to tempt the eye as well as the palate and add height to the display by using a cake stand for fruit or a table centre.

Plates don't have to match! Build up an attractive collection of china by buying appealing oddments, especially effective if you keep to a common colour or design, and increase the effect of the plates by standing them on white or border-design patterns.

What better theme for an Easter breakfast than eggs in a nest? Colourful chicks spilling out from brightly wrapped Easter eggs make an appropriate table centre which extends the idea.

FESTIVALS

Christmas and New Year's Eve settings need rich, glowing colours. Red and green are traditional colours, and there's nothing to beat swags of conifer tied with red ribbon decorating a mantelpiece or swathed around picture rails and doorways. The tree is the centre of attention, so keep it in tune with your colour theme, restricting decorations to red, silver or white. Water it daily and spray greenery to keep it fresh and remember to keep both away from open fires. Buy cheesecloth or curtain net to top a plain white tablecloth and catch it up with scarlet ribbon. Complete the look by tying napkins to match and make a table centre from holly and Christmas roses surrounding red or plain white candles.

If your room is modern, opt for a different interpretation, teaming silver with blue or black, green with cerise or pink with gold. Spray branches silver or black and drape them with lengths of tinsel and clear glass baubles. Make bonbon bags of co-loured net and fill them with silver- or gold-wrapped confectionery. Use plain tableware and plenty of glass and pile single coloured baubles in a dish for a simple table centre and place it on a mirror to increase its impact.

Easter and Whitsun (Pentecost) call for pastels – yellow (primrose or daffodil), pale green and blue to welcome spring. Mass daffodils and daisies in white or green china or glass vases or jugs and use softly coloured china on a plain cloth. Tie miniature Easter eggs in pastel bundles or choose tiny bunches of spring flowers to put by each place.

Autumn festivals demand stronger colours. A harvest supper needs a plain white cloth and napkins, pottery or stoneware plates and creamy candles. Make a centrepiece of fruit, piled high on a cake stand or in wood or heavy china bowls and provide vases of richly coloured roses or chrysanthemums. Hallowe'en can be sharper in black, offset by bright green, saffron and silver; remember to hollow out a pumpkin for a Jack o' Lantern and provide a large bowl filled with apples for apple-bobbing. In the UK Bonfire Night is a moveable feast – use wooden or red plastic trays to carry hot drinks and snacks outside and a create a warm welcome indoors with a winter barbecue, hot punch and red candles. In the US Thanksgiving calls for a traditional cornucopia centrepiece, set off by earth tones to complement the feast of turkey, yams and cranberry sauce.

LIFE EVENTS

Christenings are followed by a table set for tea. It's a formal occasion, so use a lace or damask cloth and fine or bone china, picking out a colour in the china to use for ribbons looped through lace or tying up 'confetti', the traditional net parcels of sugar almonds presented to guests at a baptism. Flowers should be light and fresh; choose cream and blush pink rosebuds for a girl, white daisies, campanula and forget-me-nots for a boy. Set out the spread on co-ordinating china plates, provide fine flutes for champagne and use a cake stand.

Weddings are more public affairs. Even if the reception is held away from home, consider creating a centrepiece and decorating the tables to add a personal touch. In a village or club hall, use screens or battens (slats) stapled with lengths of cheapest net or cheesecloth to create atmosphere and cover plain white sheeting with net, lace or voile caught up with satin ribbon. Use simple white china and silver cutlery and blend white with cream and tea rose for flower arrangements.

Anniversaries impose their own colour theme. Silver can be one of the prettiest, and you could create a scheme mingling silver with grey and white for an elegant effect. Choose silver candlesticks with tapering white candles and decorate the table with silver-leaved plants.

Ruby involves tints of red, from rose white to burgundy. Choose a soft pink topcloth over deep rose or burgundy, with napkins to match the lower cloth tied with pale pink ribbon. Use bone china decorated with roses and silver cutlery, and serve pink champagne in cut crystal glasses.

Gold deserves special attention. Spray net gold to swathe a cake or table centre and place on a table covered by a white damask cloth. Use lace-edged napkins tied with gold ribbon, gold-rimmed china and crystal glass, and put tiny white parcels tied with gold thread by each place. Finish with stately white flower arrangements for table centres, brass candlesticks and slim white candles.

A table made from packing crates, painted brilliant yellow, and covered by a matching wooden top, sets the scene for this buffet party. Paper plates and cups and even food and drink in the same colour add impact to the setting.

CARING FOR TABLEWARE

Those two modern conveniences, the dishwasher and microwave, are suitable for most types of china and glass with a few exceptions.

Don't use gilt-edged china in a microwave cooker as the metal will cause 'arcing' and may damage the casing.

Remember that using heavy pottery rather than plastic or glass may increase microwave cooking times.

Wash gilt-edged china on the gentlest programme setting (under 60°C) *if recommended by the manufacturer* and choose your detergent with care. If in doubt, hand wash.

Hand wash old or hand-painted china.

Check the recommendations for washing cutlery with bone, wood or plastic handles. Hand wash if necessary.

Wash delicate items and plastic on the top shelf of the dishwasher.

Do not mix stainless steel and silver in the dishwasher as silver cleaning solutions tarnish the 'stainless' steel.

Hand wash crystal and fine glass as glasses washed in a dishwasher appear milky in time.

When hand washing, begin with items that are least dirty (glasses and cutlery), then progress to plates, casseroles and saucepans, changing the water when necessary. Use a soft brush to clean cut glass and fluted china.

PLACE SETTINGS

Are you mystified by etiquette? Most of the 'rules' about laying the table have evolved for practical reasons, though there is undeniably a snob element in getting it right. If this bothers you, the first thing to remember is that what is done in restaurants may not be acceptable in the best circles. Technically, you should not, for example, lay the spoon and fork nose to tail above the dinner plate, fold napkins elaborately, serve salt in a shaker, use fish knives and forks at any time, serve soup in bowls rather than on plates at dinner or produce any food or drink in the container in which it was bought! If you are more concerned that the family should actually sit down to eat and use at least some of the cutlery provided you may be inclined to dismiss this, but such knowledge does come in useful if you have to give an important dinner for your boss or arrange a wedding reception.

Allow at least 24 inches (60 cm) table space for each person and lay the place setting in the order in which each piece of cutlery is used, so that the soup spoon is on the outside, the dinner knife and fork next and the dessert spoon and fork on the inside. Glasses should be arranged in a similar manner, with a sherry glass (if used) on the inside right of each place, small glasses for white wine and large

The 'rules' about table settings should not be taken too seriously, but they can be useful if you're involved in arranging an important formal meal. For ordinary entertaining, an informal arrangement will usually fit the bill.

glasses for red behind and a goblet for water and a champagne flute (if provided) at the back. The side plate should be on the left of each place and salt should be served in a small dish with a miniature spoon. (Pepper can be served in a medium-sized mill.) Protect your table by using thick felt beneath the cloth or table mats.

ON THE SHELF

Don't forget the decorative potential of china and glass. It's a shame to shut tableware away between meals, so consider showing dinner and tea services in glass-fronted display cupboards or on shelves, hanging decorative dinner plates on the walls and using dishes and bowls for plants or pot-pourri. Plant winter bulbs in a deep china basin and fill jugs with fresh or dried flowers. Use attractive saucers as soap dishes and hoard glass perfume bottles and toiletry jars so that you can decant supermarket best buys into prettier containers and display them on bathroom shelves.

Old tableware is still readily available, and jumble (rummage or garage) sales are often as good a source as antique shops. It won't cost much to build up a substantial collection, and what else can be put to such practical use? Ignore the quest for rare porcelain, forget about collecting sets (second-hand dinner services inevitably have some pieces missing) and concentrate on collecting pieces with a common colour or decorative theme. Imagine the impact of a table laid in blue and white with co-ordinating table linen, or a cabinet filled with pink and gold china. Link pieces with the same motif, such as roses, strawberries or bows. Mix old decorative pieces (like tureens and bowls) with new, and supplement any gaps in a table setting with plain white china.

Similarly, buying glass second-hand is the ideal way to acquire crystal on the cheap. You'll rarely find more than three or four matching goblets, but varying the styles adds to the interest of the collection. When glass is not in use, display it where the light will make it sparkle, and use uplighters and spots to show it to best effect.

You may well find that you develop a serious interest in collecting, and if the assortment is varied, the addition of, say, original Georgian or cranberry glass will only add to its effect. You may start to specialize in a certain period – Art Deco and fifties china, for example, are both of interest to collectors now – or you may prefer to concentrate on textiles such as linen or lace.

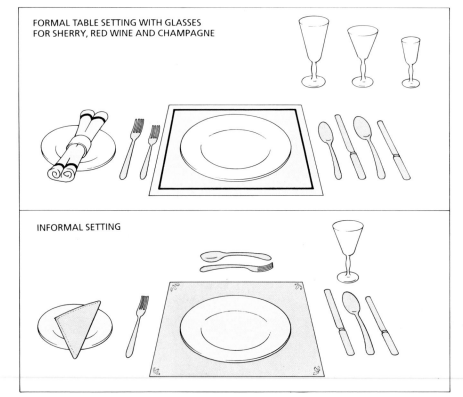

FORMAL TABLE SETTING WITH GLASSES FOR SHERRY, RED WINE AND CHAMPAGNE

INFORMAL SETTING

Too few pictures? then use patterned china plates for display, a practical choice for steamy areas like bathrooms and kitchens. Place glass high up where it reflects the light, for added sparkle.

FACESAVERS

• Make place cards to suit the theme for children's parties to prevent arguments.

• Use holders of different sizes so that candles are varied in height – but not too high to inhibit conversation – for a graceful table centre.

• Keep table centres low to encourage conversation. You can allow yourself more leeway on buffet tables, of course.

• Avoid heavily perfumed flowers.

• Make a circular table centre from chicken wire and florists' foam, stud it with candles and cover it with greenery and flowers to suit the occasion – holly, berries and red candles at Christmas, blush pink roses, gypsophila and white candles for a romantic dinner.

• Flick cheap wine glasses or white plates with enamel paint, using a toothbrush, to create a co-ordinated set: handwash only.

• Use net and ribbon to swathe a simple iced cake and turn it into a celebration special.

• Not enough matching china? Mix and match plain primary or pastel colours for an interesting modern setting, use plain white to eke out traditional designs, or alternate plain white with patterned place settings.

• Use ribbon to decorate a plain cloth, napkins or place mats and draw them into the scheme.

• If your tableware is uninteresting, concentrate on the table centre. Scatter extra flower heads over the side plates and fasten them to napkins.

• Use plain white plates beneath those in use to form a frame and add height.

• Use reflective materials, such as mirror, metallic textiles and glass, for a modern look.

CHAPTER 15

Living decor

Your house and garden are in harmony because while the house is all angles and straight lines, the garden is composed of curves and irregular shapes. We need the same variety of shapes indoors to prevent the decor from looking cold and mannered. Flowers and plants can be appreciated on their own, as part of a room scheme, or for their perfume. Like pictures, they look best en masse. Group green plants in a corner or by a window, taking care to vary the heights and never be stingy with cut flowers. Pack an arrangement with greenery or branches of blossom if there are too few choice blooms and use dried or silk flowers to brighten up your home in winter when fresh flowers are expensive, uninteresting and scarce.

FLOWERS

Fresh flowers are now available at a reasonable price for most of the year. They bring such life and freshness to a room that they should not be re-garded as an occasional luxury; even if your budget is limited, you should be able to find a cheerful inexpensive bunch within your means.

SHAPE

The best shape for general use is a dome, with the tallest flowers in the centre and shorter blooms on the outside. Avoid tall, narrow containers which won't allow the blooms to spread, and cut the stems short so that the flower heads mass together. This is also good advice for table centres, as the arrangement has no 'back', but remember to keep the arrangement low. Tall arrangements should be placed where they will look most impressive – on a chest or side table, against a window or mirror, or even filling a fireplace. You will need a container which has sufficient height to balance the arrangement and enough depth to support it. Aim for a pyramid effect by placing tall spires in the centre and graduate the shape by selecting shorter flowers

One colour and white makes for foolproof flower arrangements, especially if the colour relates to one that's dominant in the furnishings, as here. Blue and white are repeated in the colours of the wide container which allows the flowers to fan out.

to form a graceful cone.

There's a place for every size of arrangement. Modest posies will freshen up a cloakroom or bedroom, while sheafs of herbs and grasses look appropriate in a kitchen. The modern trend is towards arrangements which look casual and natural rather than forced, so don't attempt to torture flowers into an elaborate shape. Use a wedge of florists' foam (make sure it protrudes above the rim of a bowl or shallow platter to give the arrangement height) and chicken wire to support large sprays, or arrange flowers so that they support each other, with strong, upright blooms at the centre and delicate ones on the outside. For impact, use a single type of flower such as tulips, which bend elegantly, roses, or marguerites.

COLOUR

One-colour arrangements are foolproof! Nothing looks fresher than a blend of white blooms against a background of greenery, but tints of one colour – pink hydrangea heads with pink roses and mauve-pink stocks, for example – look equally effective. You can also choose colours which relate (such as orange and yellow) or which are complementary, or opposite each other on the colour wheel. Some colours provide you with a ready-made colour scheme. Think of Michaelmas daisies with their 'complementary' scheme of purple-blue blooms with yellow centres or sweet peas in relating tones of lavender and mauve. Avoid multi-coloured arrangements where the colours are similar in strength and remember that the arrangement should contribute to its setting, co-ordinating or contrasting, but not clashing with your colour scheme.

VARIETIES

Roses, carnations, daffodils and chrysanthemums are what everyone thinks of as 'cutting' flowers but you can achieve interesting effects with many others. Think about campanula, larkspur, Livingstone daisies, scabious, and gypsophila, whose tiny white flowers are invaluable for adding softness to an arrangement. Don't forget flowering shrubs like the fragrant philadelphus, Mexican orange, forsythia and lilac which will bulk out an arrangement. (Crush the base of the stems to increase their life.) You can use this type of plant in conjunction with berries, like holly and cotoneaster, or interesting foliage, like many hostas, eucalyptus and eleagnus, to add interest when flowers are scarce and therefore expensive to buy.

Above: Flowers everywhere – the effect of this group owes as much to the rich floral pattern of the cloth and china as to the dahlias, lilies, pelargoniums and hydrangea heads which fill them.

Left: All-white arrangements have an elegant simplicity. Arrange flowers informally in a plain white vase and group with other white ceramics, like the candlesticks shown here, for maximum effect.

VASES

Use jugs, bowls or dishes as well as the purpose-made variety. For versatility, look for wide containers rather than tall narrow shapes which make it difficult to manipulate the blooms. Vases can be chosen to put the focus on the flowers (clear glass,

Flowers and herbs hung to dry are part of the traditional country kitchen. Use ready-dried flowers in wicker baskets suspended from wooden poles for decoration.

pottery or white china, for example) or to add decorative impact. Stippled or crackled glaze vases in soft colours can blend with the room scheme, patterned jugs and china bowls add a decorative note, while plain china in vivid colours, grey or black is ideal for modern arrangements; try placing red tulips in a purple vase or daffodils in a black one, for example. You'll find 'flat' vases, jokey ones shaped like paper bags and others decorated with fruit or bows. Indeed, it's no longer necessary to put flowers in vases, for one modern trend is to group empty vases for display – china ones in relating colours, or glass ones, which reflect the light, in interesting variations of shape and size.

CARING FOR CUT FLOWERS

Cut flowers are a beautiful addition to any home, but they can be an expensive luxury if you don't have a garden which can provide blooms all the year round.

Cut flowers at an angle to increase their life. You should also soak flowers in deep, tepid water for several hours before they are arranged and strip any leaves from the base of the stems so that they don't foul the water.

Bleach the container to kill bacteria and rinse it well before filling with water. Use a cut flower preservative to extend the life of your arrangement and position flowers in a cool place. Change the water every few days and recut the stems each time.

DRIED OR ARTIFICIAL FLOWERS

These are widely available and have the considerable advantage of lasting all year round.

Dried flowers can be bought or alternatively you can dry blooms from your garden, hanging them upside down in a dry, cool room. Opt for flowers which have naturally papery petals, like hydrangea and poppies, add seedheads and pods like honesty and clematis and complete with dried grasses. Choose wide containers (baskets are ideal) filled with florists' foam, and display them away from strong sunlight to preserve their colours.

'Silk' flowers (usually made from polyester) are permanent, expensive and realistic. They are particularly easy to arrange because the stems are made from covered wire which twists into place and they can be washed in cool detergent solution when necessary.

PLANTS

Most garden centres, nurseries and some large supermarkets have a good selection of indoor plants, ranging from the fragile and exotic to the hardy and common. Bear in mind where you want your plant to live; buying a plant which likes plenty of sun when the room you want it to decorate is dark can be an expensive mistake. Don't neglect growing your own from edibles; pineapple and avocado are easy to grow and make attractive and delightful plants.

DISPLAYING PLANTS

Houseplants add year-round greenery and pay decorative dividends for remarkably little attention. To ensure that they contribute to the decor, make sure they are healthy and banish those that are ailing until they are fit to be seen. Group plants for maximum impact, in a corner, on a table or by a window. Group flowering plants like impatiens on a step, place climbers where they can wind naturally round window frames or banisters and give interest to the ceiling with hanging baskets of trailing ferns. You'll need to vary the heights within a group and remember that plinths, low tables and traditional jardinières will give prominence to large single plants. Use mirrors to increase the impact of an arrangement and disguise an unpleasant view by placing sun-loving plants or pots of herbs on glass shelves across the window, eliminating the need for curtains or blinds. Choose plants with delicate leaves and an open appearance as they look less stiff than those with spiky or glossy leaves.

Most plants flourish in the light, provided they are shaded from the glare of the sun. Shelves fixed across a window allow these plants to create a living screen while the tins used as planters make attractive and unusual containers.

CHOOSING PLANTS

Centrally heated houses impose a special stress on houseplants because they have to adapt to a constant temperature all year round, although some may thrive on this. Make sure the atmosphere is sufficiently humid by raising the plant on pebbles above water or spraying it, if the species permits. Look at *Dieffenbachia, Dracaena marginata, Ficus benjamina, Peperomia* (the watermelon plant), *Scindapsus aureus* and the Kentia palm. Ivies and tradescantias like cool conditions, so they are ideal for occasionally used rooms and halls – but no plant likes draughts. Dark corners are another problem. The aspidistra is one plant which will tolerate dismal conditions, as will many ferns, though they need shade rather than absence of light. For full sunlight you'll need pelargoniums and cacti; other varieties will frizzle up in the direct glare of the sun.

PLANTERS

Unfortunately, the pots in which plants are bought are far from lovely, so you will need to buy planters. Because drainage is essential it's often easier to conceal the flowerpot inside a decorative planter, though it is possible to buy planters with drainage holes and separate saucers if you prefer. Choose planters to reflect the style of your room – fine patterned china for a traditional scheme, speckled earthenware for a sophisticated modern one, wicker for a more casual style. Press decorative chamber pots and basins into service and place large plants in waste paper baskets or painted garden tubs. Small plants look pretty in jugs, mugs or brass or wooden boxes. Use plastic planters with care: primary colours suit a bright modern setting but avoid unconvincing imitations of ceramic or wood, which never quite work.

CHAPTER 16

The personal touch

If you have ever moved house, or cleaned out an attic, you will have been amazed at the number of things you have stowed away. They range from favourite photos which were put in a box 'for now', to pieces of glass and china, pictures which need cord or hangers, textiles, trays and collections of anything from postcards to old magazines. They are of too much personal value to throw away, and of not enough merit to display in their present condition, yet these are the things which stamp a room with individuality. What should you do?

Right: Turn your hobby to decorative effect. This collection of painted eggs is piled into a plain glass vase; an alternative would be to display them in a stained egg rack or china egg cups.

Below: Use shelves, hooks and plate racks to assemble a collection of china and keep everyday pieces close at hand. Fill the gaps with cuttings, postcards or other ephemera to form an ever-changing display.

The answer is to package them so that the presentation adds distinction to the contents. Frames are an obvious solution, not only for flat objects but for 3-D ones too. This is a particularly effective way of displaying a collection, whether it's of photographs, postcards, magazine covers, anniversary or birthday cards, dried flowers, fans or pieces of lace. Arrange postcards or photographs on a single mount, or cut them to form a collage. Pin textiles to a contrasting coloured backing and finish with a box frame, but don't use non-reflective glass here as the distance between the glass and the backing will make the contents seem blurred.

Larger objects like pieces of china and glass should be displayed on shelves or plate hangers. Find uses for single items as impromptu vases, soap dishes, or sugar bowls. Sort out the contents of your cupboards from time to time with a view to deciding what can be used for display. A handsome tray, for example, can be hung on the wall while an old coffee pot or jug can be filled with flowers instead of being hidden away.

Everyday items as well as treasures can be used for decoration. Turn out the kitchen drawers and see if the *batterie de cuisine* wouldn't look better, and be closer to hand, hung from hooks or racks on the wall or suspended from the ceiling via butcher's hooks on a steel pole. Baskets can be hung from curtain poles across the ceiling, filled with dried flowers and interspersed by bunches of herbs hung to dry, to create a country kitchen atmosphere. Store pots and casseroles on open shelves or even stack them on the floor to make the most of their looks. Fill shelves with items which are nice to look at as well as those which are taken down and used – whether books or dishes – because rows of shelves look better with a mixture of contents to add visual variety. Make sure that things in regular use are kept separate from the ornaments and are easily taken down and put back again, otherwise you'll be in constant danger of the whole arrangement toppling down and causing breakages.

When displaying items on one shelf, treat it as a single arrangement. Balance a clock or bookends at one end by a candlestick, painting and trailing plant at the other, to create a harmonious group, rather than dotting ornaments along at intervals, which jars on the eye.

Hooks and hangers are also useful and practical methods of display. Consider a key rack in the hall or an old-fashioned hallstand complete with mirror, glove box and umbrella trays. Develop the hanging basket theme for storing small items such as soaps, ribbons or kitchenware.

Try to visualize how furniture can be used in a different context. Drape a bentwood coatstand with scarves and hats to make a focal point in the bedroom, or use stout wicker hampers as bedside tables. Industrial storage baskets and the domestic equivalent are often available in bright primary colours. Use the tiny wall-mounted containers intended for screws and washers for kitchen paraphernalia instead, or for bits and pieces in a high-tech study or sewing room. Colourful stacking baskets are efficient ways of keeping together shoes, sports gear or children's toys.

Finally, what about the items which you don't want on show? You can decant foodstuffs like coffee and flour into attractive containers and use soap and cosmetics decoratively but the cornflakes, shoe polish and toothpaste are best hidden from view – and, of course, you'll need wastebins. Provide sufficient cupboards, boxes and storage units to contain all the things you want to shut away and allow one 'temporary' container in each room for goods in transit. A linen chest in the hall, clothes basket in the bathroom or bedroom and a decorative box in the living room will take everything you collect in that quick blitz which takes place before visitors descend. The variety of storage systems available has improved greatly in recent years, and there is sure to be a type to suit your home and family. Even strong cardboard boxes could be pressed into service – in a child's room cover them with wrapping paper and use to store favourite toys. Removing what's not attractive is the other side of the coin to planning the perfect finishing touch, but it's just as vital to the smart and well thought-out appearance of your home.

If you hoard it, flaunt it. This 'speculative' collection is appropriately displayed above a bureau, where it forms part of a group defined by the pictures and pocket watches each side.

FACESAVERS
- Loathe to part with paperbacks or old books? Cover them with marbled wrapping paper (or marble your own) for an attractive display.
- A cupboard that's lost its door can be wall-mounted and used for display. Paint the inside a colour which relates with the decor.
- A printer's tray upended and hung on the wall makes a splendid container for showing off tiny china ornaments.
- Create a novelty clock by fixing a quartz movement to plywood cut in a simple rectangle, abstract or animal shape and painted or stained in bright colours.
- Attractive containers can be filled with pot pourri to both scent and decorate a room.

Glossary of design terms

Art Deco Prominent style in the decorative arts of the 1920s and 1930s, characterized by solid shapes and lines, vivid colours and new man-made substances such as plastics.

Art Nouveau A decorative style prominent in all visual arts throughout Europe and the USA at the end of the 19th and beginning of the 20th century. It was characterized by designs based on plant foliage, natural flowing shapes and curved lines.

Bauhaus A German school of design, and an important influence on 20th-century art from the 1920s onwards. Designers of the school sought to produce a synthesis of all arts to develop a style suitable for the industrial 20th century. Tubular steel furniture and a simple geometric style.

Breuer, Marcel Lajos (1902-81) A US designer and architect born in Hungary who taught at the Bauhaus in the 1920s and practised architecture in the USA after 1937. He designed the first tubular steel chair in 1925 and the "Wassily" chair made of nine pieces of tubular steel with leather or canvas seat, back and arm rests.

Butler tray A small collapsible portable table for carrying tea items. The top often has flaps which hinge upwards to prevent the contents falling off.

Cheval mirror An upright, centrally hinged dressing-mirror for standing on a table.

Chippendale, Thomas (1718-79) English cabinet-maker who introduced an Anglicized version of French rococo designs of the Louis XV style. Later he developed a fine neo-classical style.

Coalport A type of porcelain, from the factory founded by John Rose in 1795. Glazed bone china and fine white porcelain employing willow-pattern and transfer prints, also work in the neo-classical style with rich colours such as maroon and gilded ornamental ware encrusted with flowers.

Cranberry glass Red stained glass used especially in wine goblets, popular in the 19th century. Simple goblets with a clear stem and red bowl.

Crown Derby Porcelain first introduced by William Duesbury (1725-86). Decorated in bold blues and reds and gilt 'Japan' patterns, also depicting landscapes and plant illustrations.

Davenport A small desk dating from around 1830 to the end of the century, a feature of which was that the main drawers opened to the side.

Gateleg A style of table dating from the late 17th century with flaps supported on hinged gate-like supports which allowed it to be collapsed and stored flat.

Georgian British architectural style of the reigns of George I to George IV (1714-1830), based on classical Roman architecture and art. Characterized by well-proportioned elegance, especially in domestic architecture, with the symmetrical use of 12-paned sash-cord windows.

Gothic Art and architecture of Europe from the mid-12th century to the end of the 15th. The style is characteristic of many English cathedrals. Revived in the 19th century by the Victorians as symbolic of religious virtue.

Hepplewhite, George (?-1786) An English furniture designer who took contemporary neo-classical designs and made them simpler and more functional. The style often uses inlaid mahogany or satinwood and chairs often have heart- or oval-shaped backs and straight tapering legs.

High-tech A design style current from the late 1970s onwards, also known as 'industrial style' and 'hard edge'. Employs spare, plain, undecorated forms with sharp angles and solid colours rather than patterns, and metal, plastic and rubber rather than natural materials.

Le Corbusier, Charles-Edouard Jeannoret (1887-1965) A French architect born in Switzerland. Before the Second World War he pioneered a Cubist-influenced form of design; later he was identified with tubular steel and leather chairs and especially chaises-longues.

Liberty Liberty and Co. was founded in 1875 by Arthur Lasenby Liberty (1843-1917). Originally a warehouse and retail shop in Regent Street, London, dealing in oriental goods and fabrics, it later included porcelain and furniture and then gold and silver in the 1890s. Liberty designs were typical of the Art-Nouveau movement.

Mackintosh, Charles Rennie (1868-1928) A Scottish designer and architect, responsible for the interiors of various Glasgow tea-rooms with elaborate penduline chandeliers. Designer of simple linear perpendicular chairs with distinctive, much-copied, high backs, also cabinets with prominent brass hinges and decorative Art-Nouveau-influenced designs in brass and stained glass.

Maw and Co. Manufacturers of earthenware vases and tiles, characteristically cream with strong natural patterns.

Memphis A design style of the 1980s, based on outrageous shapes and colours. This design school emerged partly as a reaction to the stark sterility of modernism and also to undermine the sophisticated Italian classical look evident in the 1970s.

Morris, William (1834-96) An English designer, artist, writer and poet. He started a firm of decorators and designers (Morris and Co.) in 1861, placing the emphasis on pre-industrial crafts and natural forms in stained glass, carpets, furniture and especially fabric and wallpaper designs.

Mintonware Porcelain produced at the pottery founded by Thomas Minton (1765-96) in Stoke in 1796. It still produces fine porcelain and brilliantly painted tiles and statues.

Mondrian, Piet (1872-1944) A Dutch painter. After 1917 his abstract paintings developed a style comprising horizontal and vertical lines, primary colours, black and white. This style, known as neo-plasticism, influenced the Bauhaus school.

Neo-classicism A movement in art and architecture dominant in Europe between 1750 and 1850, involving a revival of classical art and architecture. It developed under the stimulus of the Enlightenment as a reaction to the frivolity of the rococo style. Both the Georgian and Regency styles are related to it.

Pembroke A small table first made in the 1760s, associated especially with Sheraton. Typically it has two hinged flaps and a drawer and stands on slender, tapered legs.

Picasso, Pablo (1881-1973) A Spanish artist of great inventiveness and versatility of style. Early in his life (1901-4) he went through a phase of painting figures in shades of blue only – his 'blue period'.

Regency An English decorative style fashionable during the reign of the Prince Regent (later George IV) from 1800-30. Furniture used dark exotic woods, was somewhat heavy, deriving influence from Roman, Greek and even Egyptian styles, and often employed oriental lacquer work.

Regency Trafalgar chair A Regency-style dining chair. It has the centre bar of the back in the nautical form of a rope and its lines are clean with back, frame and legs all flush at the sides.

Romantic revival A trend at any time to revive the Romantic period in art of the 19th century. The Romantic period represented a reaction against neo-classicism with its emphasis on formality and containment in art, and a return to the natural and a celebration of the imagination.

Royal Worcester A soft paste porcelain first made in Worcester in about 1750. Early examples were modelled upon contemporary silver shapes and oriental porcelain, and the wares generally use transfer printing and gilding.

Sheraton, Thomas (1751-1806) An English furniture designer. Influenced by contemporary French styles, the designs are elegant and delicate and use straight lines, inlaid decoration and slender tapering legs.

Sofa table A development of the Pembroke table around the end of the 18th century, being about 5 feet long with short flaps, two drawers and a height convenient for standing beside sofas.

Spode Fine tableware and other porcelain made in the Staffordshire pottery of Josiah Spode (from 1770). Often decorated with transfer printing and painted 'Japan' patterns enhanced by gilding.

Tiffany, Louis Comfort (1848-1933) An American glass-maker and decorator, son of Charles Tiffany who founded Tiffany and Co. which specialized in silver and gold. Louis Tiffany opened a shop selling stained glass in 1895. Characteristic lamps have pottery or bronze bases with colourful stained glass mosaics on the shade. The registered trade mark of the glass is 'Favrile'.

Tudor The period of the Tudor monarchs ran from 1485-1603 and the furniture of this period was characteristically heavy, dark, usually of oak and frequently elaborately carved.

Trompe l'oeil French for 'fools the eye'. A method of painting features to create the illusion that they are real rather than painted.

Voysey, Francis Anneely (1857-1941) An English designer, architect and typographer, designer of simple upright furniture in wood with little surface decoration except prominent brass hinges and handles. His floral print designs used natural shapes and curves.

Wedgwood, Josiah (1730-95) An English potter who opened his own factory in Burslem, Staffordshire, England in 1759. The pottery popularized classical styles and designs, included creamware and jasperware and introduced transfer printing to Staffordshire.

Windsor chairs Wooden chairs of various designs sharing the feature of a solid, saddle-shaped seat from which the chairs derive their rigidity, the turned legs and spokes of the back support being driven into holes bored into it.

Index

Acknowledgments

The publishers thank the following for providing the photographs in this book:
ARCAID (Richard Bryant) 89, (Lucinda Lambton) 10; Botanical Pictures 1, 119 above; Jon Bouchier 4 right, 23, 48, 70, 95, 120; Camera Press 2-3, 5 above, 14, 37, 40, 43 right, 44, 47, 53, 69, 71, 75, 77, 80, 83, 98 left and right, 101 above, 105, 106, 107 above, 111, 113, 114, 115, 121, 123; Collier Campbell 26, 34 above and below, 60, 63 below, 81; Designers Guild 78; Good Housekeeping 15; Susan Griggs Agency 49, 72 below, 84, 90, 92 above, 96, 118; Next Interior 8, 28, 59, 73; Jessica Strang 5 below, 51, 58, 60, 61 below, 64, 65, 72 above, 76, 79, 82, 100, 107 below, 119 below, 122 above; Syndication International (Homes & Gardens) 13, 25, 88, (Options) 31, 41; Top Agence (P. Hinous) 11; Elizabeth Whiting & Associates 4 left, 12, 17, 19, 21, 22, 24, 27, 39, 42, 43 left, 45, 50, 54, 56, 61 above, 62, 63 above 67, 68, 85, 86, 87, 92 below, 93, 94, 97, 99, 101 below, 102, 103, 108, 109, 112, 117, 122 below; The World of Interiors (James Mortimer) 9, (Fritz van der Schulenburg) 29, (John Vaughan) 57, (James Wedge) 33.

The publishers are also grateful to Maire and Martin Skinner for compiling the Glossary of design terms and to Valerie Lewis Chandler, BA, ALAA for compiling the index.